How Could I Forget: Willa Wonka's Memories

Memories and Letters to
My Sweet Dear John

Part 1
A Series of Willa's Memoirs

Willa Grant

ISBN 978-1-63874-795-6 (paperback)
ISBN 978-1-63874-796-3 (digital)

Christian Faith Publishing, Inc.
832 Park Avenue
Meadville, PA 16335
www.christianfaithpublishing.com

Printed in the United States of America

Contents

Introduction

Meet Willa, the mother of now ten children, wife, author, and believer of the Almighty God!

From spiritual warfare and the depths of darkness of child abuse, child molestation, bullied by peers, outcast, became a mother of two at age seventeen, drugs, jail, prostitution, domestic abuse, rape, and death experiences.

When God says I'm not through with you yet, believe him! I am a living testimony!

One of the realizations that most people always seemed to find refreshing about me is that I don't mind being forthcoming or open about my past when asked about it. About the mistakes that I have made and experiences that I have endured which could've led me to an early grave. But there were many times that I've vented to the wrong ears about being so forthcoming about my past mistakes. Most have taken the information that I have confided in with them and have used it against me. Those certain people whom I've entrusted with only small details of bits and pieces of my past have frowned upon me like rotten meat, not only for my disadvantage but have made my words backfire against me that did more damage and harm versus good. Those same people that I thought would help me and give me hope instead threw bricks or added more shade to my darkness. I have never understood these crossfires because I really put so much trust into others, especially men.

Some of my ex-lovers have used my past experiences and mistakes that I've openly shared to them to entice my vulnerable state of mind and did their best to have control over me because they figured

I had no hope or direction in life. Those same men have made me feel like less of a person, used my past to tarnish my character, and took advantage of me. They've brainwashed me into thinking no one really cared about me and that they were my only hope, so I should follow their every command as if they were my savior.

I've lived a past life that is so shameful and usually too embarrassing to discuss with others that even I, myself, am shocked at how open I am to verbally relive my trials and tribulations with others. I was also judged and frowned upon after being open and honest to my peers about my upbringing without them really knowing the long backstory version. Something inside of me always felt compelled to explain my situations to others, but I didn't realize that most of the time, I was sharing my past with all the wrong people.

Those same gawkers couldn't last a day in my shoes if the tables were turned if they've had to live my past life. They've never known of my real, true struggles and hardships that gave me no hope at some point in my life to just be as is, with no true purpose. I thought I'd write about my story from A to Z in a four-part series to share with others who are facing their own darkness with hopes of encouraging them and that there is a God. To let them know that they are not alone and to stand in faith, trust God, and to keep pushing forward because there is light at the end of the tunnel even when everyone seems to be against you.

I was abused, shamed, and was outcast by others.

But when God is for you, who can be against you?

This first part of the memoir series is based on the upbringing of my memories and stories that describe my dysfunctional journey and experiences of my childhood. Many of my trials and tribulations have never caused me to lose my faith in God; a seed that has been planted in me which is far beyond this world that even I myself didn't understand!

I've been so trusting in God, that even when it didn't seem like I wouldn't make it through the depths of darkness, God has always pulled me through and kept me here to be able to share my story. Some may not like it, but I truly believe God sends messages through everyone and uses us in His own way, which are many, to help others be encouraged, to be inspired to put their trust in Him and not on man. I may not be a saint, but my faith is what kept me going and still keeps me going; now I feel inspired to share my story, especially to those who don't seem to see a way through even in the darkness and through the storms. "You of little faith, why are you so afraid?" Then he got up and rebuked the winds and the waves, and it was completely calm" (Matthew 8:26)

Everyone has a story and history behind them, and I want to share mine.

Here is my history.

This is my story.

August 27, 1979

My life started off like a roller-coaster ride. I hadn't been ejected out of my mother's womb yet but was within a matter of seconds to be on a thrill ride of my life to the outside world. I guess I couldn't wait any longer to see what the world had in store for me, so I ended up being received by two paramedics in the back of an ambulance. I was in such a rush to get here to this God-given Earth that I couldn't resist another waiting moment for my mother to make it in time for the delivery ward to be able to push me out of her womb in a hospital bed. The labor actually started at my mother and father's home in West Oakland, California. My parents were already blessed with other children, their two daughters that they were raising which were my two older sisters.

Luckily for me and my sister, God had blessed my mother and father with my eldest sister, who was always a great help for my mother. When my father wasn't home, my oldest sister was of great help and company for my mother while keeping an extra eye out on my other sister. She also was of great help because she also kept a close eye out on my mother during her last month of pregnancy with me. When my mother went into labor with me, my oldest sister followed every instruction from my parents to call for help when the time came because she wanted to ensure our mother's health and my (her new baby sister's) safety. She was such a mature child for her age.

Being born in an ambulance was also our family's only resort for me since neither my mother or father owned a vehicle at that time. Not having a family car back then was a blessing in a good sense because I had rather been born in the back of an ambulance with a medical crew besides being in the back of a non-emergency vehicle. The medical security that was present helped secure that my mother and I would be in the best of care just in case something were to go wrong with my mother's labor. In the evening hours of August 27, 1979, my oldest sister called 911 and requested that medical emergency assistance be sent to our home because our mother was in so much pain from her water being ruptured.

Get Me Out of Here...
I'm Ready, Mom!

Breathe, Mommy...you can do it! Push! Push! One more push! Even though we're almost at the hospital, Mommy, I just can't wait to see you! Let me out of here! I want to see what this "outside world" thing is all about that God created! Come on, Mommy, with this fourth last push and push me out already! And voila! It's a tiny, beautiful, and healthy baby girl! I had finally been ejected from my mother's womb and born on the corner of Ashby Street in Berkeley, California. If I had only been a little less anxious and stubborn in my mother's womb, I could have actually had a normal hospital delivery. My precious tiny body couldn't wait for my thrill ride; therefore, I rushed myself from my mommy's womb just a couple of street blocks too soon. The hospital I would have been delivered in (that we eventually arrived to) was called Alta Bates Medical Center in Berkeley, California. There at the hospital, I weighed in at an even perfect five pounds. My mother's third perfect little baby girl whom she could spoil with love, peace, and undivided attention for at least a few nights. My mother gave all her children a middle name from one of her relatives or from our father's relatives in which I eventually followed suit when I became a mother. She named my middle name after her youngest sister's middle name who was the youngest child of their mother and father's thirteen children. My mother was the oldest of my grandfather and grandmother's thirteen children.

Oops...Hospital Is Not Home?

Alta Bates Medical Center was my second home after I abandoned my first residency in my mother's womb. The hospital became my second favorite home, but this new home was Earthbound, and my second home only lasted just a couple of days. I left my hospital home and went to my new home that was located in West Oakland, California, where I can say life was blissful, full of peace, love, and joy up until I was a little over two years old because we had to relocate to a different environment due to my parents budget of living. My parents were raising me and my two older sisters, and we were now living in a cheap hotel on Ninety-Fourth of MacArthur Avenue, which was located in the east part of Oakland. My father mainly worked graveyard shift jobs and was usually gone at night. My mother would usually take us girls over to my grandmother and grandfather's house in East Oakland, California, for the evening times to visit and have supper. We were a unit of four that would frequent with our mother's family as a daily routine while living at the hotel. Her family consisted of her mother, father, twelve siblings, and one of her sister's had two sons.

Here we all were, a large family altogether for those visiting moments in a large two-story, four-bedroom house that had two bathrooms, a den area, and two living rooms that would now be ready to welcome a new surprise family member. The new family member was going to be a great surprise for me. I was about to have a new friend close to my age which would give me a sisterly bonding responsibility to cherish. In other words, a new surprise for me in the form of a brand-new baby sister whom I could now help love and bond within the same way my older sisters had been doing with me. My little sister's birth will always be extra special for me because she was born the very next day after my second birthday. This assured me that I would always have a close best friend.

My mother went into labor on my second birthday, and again, I found myself riding inside of an ambulance during her pregnancy. I was having a baby sister as a birthday gift from God to me, and I was happy that I'd get to finally be a big sister. Once the paramedic was informed of this special significant ambulance ride, he was nice enough to let me ride in the front seat, showed me how the switches for the sirens worked, and gave me my favorite snack, chocolate chip cookies. Out of all the siblings, I was the only one who had the privilege to ride with my mom and see my sister's birth at the hospital, so our bond is extra special even to this very day. We sometimes feel like twin sisters since her birthday is just the very next day after mine.

A Little Bit of Daddy and Mommy's History

Three weeks after the birth of my little sister, my father and mother wanted to relocate and move our family from the motel to another hotel that was close by the lake called Lake Merritt. That hotel was close to downtown Oakland, which was in the heart of Oakland and close to all things business. My parents wanted to keep us as an intact one-unit family that didn't have to live with other relatives in spite of the living arrangement. The location of that hotel was great because it was a roof over our heads, but it was definitely not one of the best hotels to live in at that time. It was known for a lot of drug trafficking and prostitution activity. As time went on, I noticed a big change in my dad's ways and behaviors. My father had some serious secretive control issues going on within himself. His abusive and controlling ways were becoming a part of his new daily routine outwardly. Afterwards, he became physically and emotionally abusive toward my mother.

I believe my father had relapsed from a mental trauma that he suffered from as an unfortunate result from when he served and fought in the Vietnam War. Drugs also played a part in his trauma and mental well-being which caused him to make very bad decisions. At times, he'd also become a very violent person toward my mother or anyone standing in his way. While fighting during the Vietnam War, my father and other soldier members were provided hardcore street narcotics from other army personnel as a way to cope with the casualties, stresses during the war while on duty in helping with protecting our country. Once he finished his mission with that war, he went back home trying his best to cope with the normal world and live a normal life as much as possible. While trying to cope with the post-traumatic stresses of his combative experiences, my father came back home to the states to attend a college and joined a singing band. My father had two other children prior to meeting my mother. His first wife had my first half-sister and his second wife had my oldest half-brother. When he met his first two wives, he was in a singing group called the Numonics. His passion was singing, and he always wanted a stable big family that he could call his own. He was usually in and out of rehab during those times. My father's first two marriages eventually failed, but he ended up meeting my mother in East Oakland when he lived around the corner from her. He played college football and turned his life around with high hopes of change for a normal, better life.

When my mother and father first met, he was friends with my mother's brothers, and then after a little while later, they were introduced to each other. My mother was not always a city girl. Unlike my father, she was a country girl from down south, Baton Rouge, Louisiana. Growing up back then in Louisiana was so very restricted from having close access to a city. She grew up deep in the woods, forest-like, that one would call it the boondocks. Whenever she had to go to a store, it was a six-mile walk there and back. Their home bathrooms were located outside of the house called the outhouse, and there were always juke joints nearby. She barely saw any parts of a city as she was always overprotected by her parents. They didn't want her to deal with or have access to city life because they were always afraid of the fast-paced dangers that the city life possessed. My mother and her sister who was next in age to the oldest always helped in raising their younger siblings as there were a total of thirteen of them.

My mother's father and mother went out on dates to the juke joints nearby almost every weekend. She and her sister had to take care of the home and watch over all the other children. They were always curious about the outside party life but were never exposed to it. My grandfather worked as a city worker in Baton Rouge and was dedicated to his job to provide for his family. He didn't believe in the welfare system; he worked full-time, five days a week, and enjoyed his weekends with his family. He also grew vegetables and raised chickens as extra food supply for his family. My grandmother was a homemaker who took care of the home, raised the children, and prepared wonderful home-cooked meals for her family daily.

My mother was their oldest child, their prize possession, who helped hold down the home, helped greatly with the other children, and did farm work as well. She helped her mother love and raise her siblings as her own. All this country life was wonderful for her but, at the same time, boring and bland some days. They had a bunch of relatives in Louisiana. My mother had a boy cousin who used to frequent my grandparents' property. He also used to come snooping around lusting after my mother and her sister. He tried a few times to have sex with my mother, but she always declined. My mother was so relieved and happy when she found out that her parents were deciding to move to the Northern States. They wanted to make that change to give their children a better quality of life and wanted to try out something different from what they were living. My mother loved the whole idea of not having to tend to the farm anymore, walking miles just to make a store run, being annoyed by her male cousin, worrying about the tornadoes and swamp areas trapped with quicksand puddles, and being around new different people. She started to long for the day that they hit the road onto their new journey and life. Traveling with a family with such a big challenge, my grandparents were willing to do that for them and their children.

My grandfather was a true hustler and had great work credentials, so finding work and making money was no hassle for him. My grandmother was extremely supportive in all of his endeavors because she trusted her husband wholeheartedly because she knew that his family meant everything to him. So they agreed, and the decision was made to make that move. My grandparents made the arrangements to find out everything they needed to learn about the Northern States. Their discovery was quite impressive, doable, and interesting. They also discovered that their daughter was pregnant, which gave them more motivation to make that transition. Once my grandparents made that discovery, they decided to move their family to Oakland, California, where they purchased a home to start their new life in a city. My grandparents were now having their first grandchild from that discovery, a grandson, and yet, they too were pregnant with their thirteenth child, the last of the bunch, a little girl!

Abuse for a While Wasn't Much of a Secret

Once in the city, my mother had a good ol' time exploring around and getting to know her newfound city. She dated a few men who were all come-and-go relationships. This one particular man she met was very manipulative, and he was able to lure my mother into his web of lies and deceit. He thought that he had my mother wrapped around his finger so tough that he took advantage of her kindness and weakness, trying to lure her into prostitution. After she realized what his intentions for their union would be about, she finally got the big picture. She really thought that guy really loved her, but once it was made clear that he didn't love her the way she hoped he did, and that he was only using her for his advantage, she made a clean escape from that strange lover. She went back home and attended college, and once she met my dad, all of her seeking, searching for a man, and dating days came to an end.

My father had been released from rehab and back at home living with his mother when the two first met. My dad was really good friends with my mother's brothers. They always played basketball together at the neighborhood parks. After my father started dating and became intimate with my mother, they got married and eventually became a complete loving family with children. Her secret life of abuse by the hands of my father happened only on his not-so-good days. There was this one situation that happened with my mother and father that caused my mother to want to end the marriage and seek refuge. He was on heavy drugs this particular instance, and she couldn't take the physical abuse anymore. My mother and father were so secretive with their arguments or fights that they hid it so well from their kids and relatives. I was so little that I had to be maybe about four years old when I witnessed my father hit my mother in their station wagon that was parked in front of my grandmother's house.

Their argument was so silent and secretive that it scared me because I thought that maybe he didn't mean to hit her but her face just so happened to be in the way of his fist! I had no idea what conspired that blow. Most never knew that they were having fights up until that very last fight that transpired and almost cost my mother her life. She didn't want to tell her parents what was going on, so she hid the marks and bruises that were on her from their fights so no one would notice them when they'd visit her relatives. My mother tried calling it quits with my dad after she escaped and took us with her to a battered women's shelter in San Francisco. That location was such a secret and discreet location that no one knew where my mother was. She made a request that legal aid would help waive and file for a divorce from my father, but that never went through because she ended up getting back with my father after my grandparents found out about her situation, whereabouts, and what was really going on.

My mother somehow was on a San Francisco TV news segment about abused women with children, and that's how her parents were able to get an idea of where she was possibly staying and what may have been going on. Their secret was no longer a secret, and the truth about the two was out there in the open.

Back at the Hotel

My mother and father were both now at this point into drugs and using together. My father on one hand was doing up to four different types of narcotics so heavily, which I'm sure had a lot to do with him going crazy and being controlling to my mom at times. My mother on another hand didn't experiment with all the drugs that my father was into, but I know the drug that he did introduce her to was crack cocaine that they both chose to indulge in together. She started using the drug as a way to escape her stress and depression from episodes of abuse. His narcotic preferences that my father chose to indulge were PCP, heroin, cocaine, and crack cocaine. By him mixing all those drugs as well with the daily doses of alcohol was a sure recipe for disaster. My father who was raised in a well-rounded family, was college-educated, handsome, and could sing his heart out like a bird, was genuinely a wonderful loving dad, but at times, he made out for a scary and abusive husband from the effects of the drugs and alcohol that he consistently consumed.

At the age of four years old, my life would be changed forever. My family was completely out of control at this point because my mother and father were getting heavily intoxicated with neighbors that were staying in the same hotel that we stayed at almost every other few days out of the week. My father was always on edge because he felt that my mother would come to her senses and seek safety again and run off with his four girls and divorce him. His anger and emotions were mostly due to him being high on drugs, pumped with liquor, mental post trauma, and thoughts running wild about his wife taking herself and children from him. His mind was all over the place, which led to his destructive behaviors and actions. My father was going through so much. He truly loved his wife, she was his world, his girls were his everything, and so his family life had just spiraled out of control. My father couldn't take much of his depression, and on this particular dark and scary day, my father's mind completely just snapped!

He was at his breaking point and needed to come up with a money scheme so that he could have other ways of scoring more drugs to help ease all of his anguish, especially since he was out of work at this point. For some strange and odd reason, my father grabbed all of his oldest three girls and lined us up against the wall, sizing us kids up as if he was preparing us for something unknown. He then pulled out a needle which had a dark liquid in it and started moving in slow motion toward us waving it around while talking to himself as if he were in deep thought but instead saying his thoughts. It all sounded like mumbles but seemed like he was asking questions and trying to make a decision. It was so hard to understand what he was really saying because he was panting, sweating, and breathing really hard as if he was practicing for a drill.

My mother's intuition woke her up out of her sleep, and she came charging at my father to save us from what seemed to her as if he were going to inject us with his drugs. That was her mother's intuition's first thought, so she fought hard to knock the needle out of his hand! After she successfully was able to distract my father, he kept trying to convince her to let him carry out his plan from the horror that he was plotting on doing to us. They began to tussle, wrestle, then it became an all-out fight and battle. The fight was almost like a tug-o-war tussle, which seemed to last forever. As my mother was yelling and screaming for help to whomever in the hotel could hear her cry now that my father is overpowering her from the hits and blows, I was in such a state of shock, that I just stood in place, numb, scared, that I cried out like a little baby because I felt hopeless and confused. I had no idea what was going on with our parents. The chaos became so obvious and noisy from the stomping and bumping into the walls that somebody who was a close associate of my mother's (who also lived in the hotel adjacent to the room next to us) heard all of the commotion going on in our room. The noise prompted her to get in touch with my uncle (he was one of her younger brothers that was a good muscle for our family), who was my mother's emergency contact. We had no telephone in our hotel room, but our neighbor who knew my mother did. In Oakland at those times, the police were highly known for not responding in a timely manner for an emergency. They took their precious time responding to a call back then, especially if the call were coming from an altercation associated in a drug-infested hotel that housed addicts. Even though my mother's friend called 911, she felt compelled to contact a family member that my mother always spoke highly of. This particular brother of my mother was always good for giving her car rides and also the type of protective brother who, in emergency situations, always looked out for all his sisters as the alpha male muscle, protection, security, and backup help.

My mother had previously written his number on her friend's (neighbor) telephone card so that she didn't lose it or just in case she couldn't memorize it and to make sure that it would be saved next to a phone. In the meanwhile, we all were waiting before my uncle and any police would show up at the hotel to help save my mother from our father. Our father at that time was a decent-sized man with a very large build. The fight between the two drastically escalated and had moved from inside the hotel room outside on to the hotel floor balcony. The balcony areas were walkways to the hotel guest rooms; ours was on the third floor of the hotel, which was located outside and three stories high. This fight had occurred in the daylight hours, so the people that knew my mother and father who also lived in the hotel on the same floor witnessed the struggle.

At that particular hotel, most of the residents and hotel visitors were drug users themselves. It was a high chance that they possibly had drugs in their possession, so the last thing that they wanted was the police being called to the hotel and coming to investigate on the property. When the police would show up at locations as such, they'll usually start looking for more crimes with their task force and drug K-9 units aside from what they were originally called for. So a few people ran to the third floor and tried to stop the action by getting involved with my mother and father's altercation by pleading with them. The neighbors tried with much effort to calm their situation before it got too destructive and out of hand. At certain moments, their peers even tried to physically get my father off of my mother when he'd have her in a headlock during the commotion. Even though they wanted to help the couple settle their matter quietly without causing no attention for the law enforcements to show up, they were all extremely intimidated by my father because he was a somewhat built, large, and strong-looking man. My father was obviously numb from the drugs he had recently administered, so any efforts to try and physically hold him down or away from my mother, probably would have had no effect on him. He then pulled out a small pocketknife from his pants pocket.

The neighbors were trying to help the fight, but they had to be very careful for themselves once they noticed the pocketknife in his hand. They did not want to get injured during the commotion, so they backed away talking to him, telling my father that it wasn't worth it and to just put the knife away. When he saw how intimidated the neighbors were, he somewhat felt that he had total control of my mother at that point during the fight because she was now tired out and out of breath. My father had this unstoppable, unforgiving, and revengeful energy because he was so frustrated with my mother because he felt that she was going to take away his family from him.

After realizing how bad the drugs were taking over his mind and the dangerous position that he put her and their children were in, especially after she witnessed what he was about to do their daughters, she kept yelling to him that she was going to take the kids and leave him. He then realized that his fears would come to life, that she would deliver on her words, he felt threatened by the fact that he would lose his family, that she would try to take her kids and leave him for good afterwards. So by him being so high on drugs and being emotionally unstable during the physical war between him and my mother, my dad really fully snapped. He decided that he would go for the kill and just take her life instead. His conclusion was that he would kill her, take his children, and take back full control of his home of how he wanted it to be. Like a crazed maniac that was so high and strung out on PCP, my poor mentally unstable, intoxicated father grabbed a knife and charged at my poor helpless mother.

He then pushed all his heavy weight into her, smashing and cornering her into the rail; he grabbed her by her hair, pulling her head back while her body was positioned halfway off the balcony rail with full access to her exposed neck with a knife in his hand. As the knife was carving slowly into my mother's neck, he was chanting and trying to reason with my mother by asking her "Why do you want to break up our family? Are you going to leave me? Why are you doing this to me?" All that my mother could do during that nightmare was cry, pray to God, and hope that he doesn't kill her. She was very afraid that she was going to lose her life at that moment. My father was completely out of his mind at that time, and no one else was successful enough to stop him. A few seconds later, my uncle appeared like a superhero out of nowhere and grabbed my father off my mother by putting my dad in a chokehold while pulling him off of my mom! Thank God for sending my uncle there to help save my mother! He was uninjured in the process. My mother was finally able to escape and could get herself and kids away safely. My father was then apprehended and arrested once the Oakland police department arrived.

My mother loved, honored, and truly followed her husband. She was very submissive, supportive, and understanding toward our father. That's why I give her a lot of love and respect 'til this very day for the courage that it took for her to rescue us that day because who knows what would have happened to us at that horrifying moment. Regardless of her high or addiction to drugs, she was conscious enough to know how much her kids meant to her and a horrible feeling that they may have been in danger. She loved her kids so much that she focused on how important prayer was at that instant. I also forgave my dad for his actions that day because I knew he wasn't his usual self. He was a great loving father who was not mentally well because he let the drugs get the best of him and take over his mind.

Great-Aunt and Uncle Helps Our Transition

After our great escape from my mother's near-death incident on the third-floor balcony, my great aunt- and uncle-in-law moved us to a duplex they owned in West Oakland. My father didn't disappear altogether after serving jail time and did try to come over a few times to my mother's new place. My mother didn't mind him seeing my sisters and I but clearly wanted nothing else to do with him. When he would pop up, she would just lock herself in the room and have us tell him that she wasn't home. He knew that she would be in the house because he knew that she wouldn't leave us in the house alone. There was one instance where I really did miss my mom and dad being together, so when he came over to visit us, I let him know where she was hiding in the room. I will never forget his chuckle and smile that day when I told him the truth. He was still respectful, calm, gave my mother her distance, and continued our hi and goodbyes.

I could tell that he wanted to get back with my mother and that he felt bad for what he did. He was so calm and happy that we were all doing well. After a while, with a few more visits, he clearly got the picture that the dissolution of their marriage was officially over. He stopped trying to pursue my mother and disappeared from the scene completely for a very long time. My mother was doing great, was finally able to get clean off drugs, and was focus on raising her children and herself.

As time went on, she had her lonely moments once we were in school, so she decided to give the dating scene a try. She had an interest in a couple of great guys that I actually liked that took her out on fancy dates and treated her children as if they were their own. They were very respectful and treated our mom as a queen. I asked my mom would she marry this one particular man who was a friend of her brother whom she was dating. He was always so fun and thoughtful of my mother that even though I was a kid, I sensed everything good about him. But ultimately, she decided to try a monogamous relationship with a guy named Bill whom she met afterwards. Now, in the beginning, Bill was okay, calm, quiet, and mostly laid-back; I thought my mother chose him only for their love connection, but later on, I found out that she was influenced by his drug connection as well as her chemistry with him.

The two did at first indulge in drug use together on a couple of days out of the week but tried to hide it well. They used to pay his cousin to babysit us, and she was fun to be around and it was fun times with her. My mother and Bill would buy a lot of fun snack foods for us to enjoy, like a little weekend party, if you will, with our babysitter to keep us occupied. We regularly visited with his family, and it was always a fun and good time. He had so many relatives that we got to meet all over Oakland. He had relatives scattered around Oakland that we would frequent that stayed in Sobrante Park, the Sixty-Fifth Village projects, and West Oakland not too far from us. My mother was never abused by Bill, and I've never seen them argue; it was always quiet and calm with the two.

I guess you could say from a drug abuse aspect, he was a saint at that time compared to my biological father. He ended up moving in with us and became the head of the household. Things didn't seem as bad as they used to be with my father because Bill didn't do drugs all the time; he was more of a functional drug user than my father. Things started to drastically change once he became the man of the house. The major heartache about having to deal with Bill as a stepfather was the consistent whippings that I endured while they were together. I used to think that he didn't like me because I was too dark-skinned and looked mostly like my father.

Everything changed in the house while Bill was in charge. I had virtually no freedom around the house anymore, and I was just locked in our bedroom that had a bathroom inside the room for almost every other day except during the times when I had to go to school and when he wasn't there. Weekends were the worst because there was no school and he'd get high on those days for his off days, so we would be just like prisoners in a room on twenty-four-hour lockdown or until further notice. In order to ensure the door would stay closed, Bill would rig a jump rope or extension telephone cord from the room door and tied the other end to the kitchen pantry door to make sure we stayed locked in the room. My mother hung out in the living room area while Bill used their bedroom for his recreational drug use. It seemed like whenever I wasn't in the room, I was given just enough freedom to get blamed for missing items in the fridge that usually resulted in an extension cord or switch lashing.

There I was, a five-year-old little girl having to endure these whippings as if I were a slave in the movie *Roots*. I knew and understood that us children do bad things all the time and need to be disciplined which may sometimes lead to a spanking. However, in my case, I would get in trouble sometimes for the things that I did and did not do, then have to go take a shower or bath to get my body wet for a brand or extension cord whipping. Bill would use different long objects to whip me all over my body, and he literally almost never missed one spot on my body. One of the most painful belts I recall was a black leather belt with silver spikes on it, but if that wasn't in his reach, then he would find something else to use or make me get a switch off the tree that was in our backyard. As the old folks would have it, this was considered normal to grab your own switch off the tree, but in my particular case, it was because Bill was either too hungover from the night before or he was being lazy to get it himself. The most ultimate extreme pain came from when I would get whippings with a telephone cord. I couldn't help but to feel helpless and hopeless in the house because I couldn't get him to like me. I couldn't just leave the house either, and I knew that my mother was going to be with him regardless because she became pregnant by him, and I felt that this was the man she planned on being committed to.

I had to endure these lashings from a man who wasn't even my father who without regret would chase me around my bedroom at five years old, wet and naked, whipping me without remorse. I used to think that he felt that what he was doing was normal and that my mother may have needed help with disciplining her children that she bore with someone else. My mother was a sweetheart and a softy. She was so kindhearted and gentle with her children even though she came from a home where discipline was stern and intact. Maybe Bill felt like I didn't respect my mother and needed to be dealt with. She didn't believe in spanking her children. I can't remember not even one time of her spanking her us. The only thing she'd do if I were being disruptive was have my oldest sister talk to me to lecture me about my behavior, which was a rarity because, for the most part, I was a good child.

I guess Bill felt that there should be some action taken without question, explanation, or the seriousness of the situation. He'd just react instantly, and it was always chaos how it went down. It didn't matter how fast I ran off or even if I hid under the bed, he would just lift the bed up like the Incredible Hulk and deliver me his punishment. It was like a war between a child and a tall grown man. Bill and my mother at some points would realize and notice how extreme my whippings were. I remember a couple times the marks and swelling were so bad that they refused to let me go to school because of the swollen welts on my arms and legs, so they would let me go play outside in the backyard instead and kept me home from school. I feared and hated Bill after so many times of these events because it just felt like he hated me first! I also yearned for the day that my mother would no longer stay involved with this man. Believe me, I wanted to give Bill the benefit of the doubt and just accept the fact that I was just a terrible five-year-old girl who deserved to be punished because of what he thought I did.

But in contrast and other situations that manifested, the lashes just kept on happening that it made me doubt that I deserved what my stepfather was doing to me. I knew in my mind and in my heart that I did nothing wrong. I was the only child in the home that received those punishments that at times I felt so singled out. At one of those times, some of the peanut butter had been missing from the peanut jar, so Bill went around and interrogated both of my older sisters, they told him that they didn't know who did it, so they thought it may have been me because they felt that he already singled me out anyway as the usual suspect. We were all clueless because we didn't know exactly who stole some of the peanut butter. So without even interrogating me or questioning me about it, he tells me to go get in the shower and run the water. He followed behind me while pulling off his belt to get ready to whip me. I took off running, and he chased me all around the room and whipped me until I couldn't move due to the soreness and stinging pain. Oh, the stings and soreness wore me out so bad that particular day that sitting down instead of laying down was my most comfortable position. I've hated peanut butter ever since.

I know a tablespoon full of missing peanut butter is a great offense when you're poor, but does the punishment really need to be that ridiculous for a little girl that you have to chase down, catch, and whip her as if she stole the rent money or something of that nature? I don't know, maybe I'm wrong, but I always felt that maybe he just didn't like me because I was dark in complexion and favored my biological father.

Yes! I Can Finally Get a Break!

My mother had contemplated a break apart from Bill a few times and was mentioning that she was possibly going to break up with him after that last event even while being pregnant with his child. Once she mentioned this possible break up with Bill because of his now obvious behaviors toward me and that he was no longer working, he momentarily stopped using drugs. Everything in the house for a few weeks was so normal and calm. We all even watched television together as a whole and enjoyed our family quality time. He didn't want to get kicked out of the house and lose my mother's love for him, so he played the role and went back into his calm shell. That lasted a good few weeks, but he relapsed, started getting high again, and we saw his old ways coming back which made her more cautious and more protective for me. I'll never forget the time when it was about midday, the house was totally quiet, clean, and Bill, out of nowhere, just decided I needed a whipping for no reason. What made this time for my punishment different was that Bill was recuperating from his drug high, so he really didn't have the energy to get out of the bed to whip me. I don't know, maybe I was being too loud or something playing in my room.

His solution to me being his problem was to have my mother whip me instead. At first, I couldn't believe that I was in trouble for nothing and was in a state of shock that my mother would actually deliver me a whipping for this man knowing that she didn't believe in spanking her children. She told me to go into her room and lay on the bed to get ready for my whipping. I closed my eyes to try and prepare for the whacks to slap on my skin, but then, when she shut her bedroom door, my mother told me to just scream every time the leather silver spiked belt hit the bed frame and to act like I was receiving my whipping. I tried to put on my best acting as I possibly could and was so relieved that my mother had defended me even if it was just by giving me a fake whipping. After our performance was over, I sat up and looked up to my mom, and we just smiled at each other because we knew for once Bill didn't get his pleasure of putting me through his famous whippings.

I think Bill thought that because my mother was pregnant with his baby it would keep her more attached and stuck with him. In actuality, my mother's pregnancy worked for my stepfather's demise. It worked out in my favor because once my mother didn't have the need nor desire for any narcotics, also, since he couldn't provide, she could really see with twenty-twenty vision toward Bill for the person that he truly was and that he was a bad habit and liability in itself! As a result of my mother coming to her senses, she was able to get the strength she needed to end that toxic relationship with him and move on with her life. She didn't immediately totally flush Bill out of her system though, he still came around from time to time for a short time thereafter but was not allowed to stay with us ever again. When he did come by to see my mother for that short period, I noticed that his urges for wanting to whip me or fault me stopped as if my mother had laid down some type of boundaries with him. Between their breakup and her putting her foot down gave me great freedom again, and all those whipping me, faulting me outburst was completely stopped and were now off-limits.

With Bill being out of the picture or at least no longer living with us, I stepped up to help my mom while she was pregnant with my baby brother. I used to enjoy going to my mother's prenatal appointments with her and always wanting to learn about how babies were made. I always noticed that my mother ate a lot of carrots and other vegetables all the time that I thought that the way that babies were made was because women who eat a lot of carrots get pregnant! My sisters and I helped our mother a lot while she was pregnant with our baby brother.

We wanted a little brother so bad that we took different adult advice to make sure that we would help our mother at home so she could have a healthy baby. I remember when we'd all walk so far to have to go to the actual grocery store. It seemed like that store was a million miles away! But we always enjoyed the walk, and we always made sure we took sit-down breaks to relax our arms from the heavy grocery bags; we'd talk, laugh, and play during those breaks. The funniest part about that walk was we would cross over this ramp where, if you would look down the gate that was on the side of you, you could see the BART train riding in different directions that was traveling through tunnels.

It was so much fun to watch! We would take a break there by standing on that walk ramp, wait to hear the BART train wheels screeching on the tracks and would be able to see the BART train operator as soon as it comes through the tunnel, yell to get the operator's attention, and they would wave at us and toot the train horn. That always made for a pleasurable walk and great quality time.

I had a newfound best friend who used to come over to play with us girls all the time, especially during the summer months. She lived across the street from us, and her parents were good friends with my mother. They made for great neighbors as well as great pals. My best friend was only allowed to play with me at my house, but I was never allowed to go play over at hers.

This one day in particular, I remember my sisters and I were concerned about my mother who was on the couch, moaning as if she was in severe pain. She had the cover over her, but it was obvious that her pain was a big deal because she was turning red, sweating, and shaking as if she were shivering. We kept asking our mother if she was okay, but she would only respond with these loud moans of pain and seemed to keep trying to find something to grab on to. It scared me so much because I thought immediately that something really bad was wrong with her. So I left the house and went across the street to knock on my best friend's (her name was Kunta Kentay) door who lived directly across the street. She was my first white female friend that I had at that time. Her parents were hippies, and they were really strange people, but very nice, welcoming, and supportive at most times. We always questioned why we couldn't play over at Kunta Kentay's house, but I then saw why when I went over to her house to use their phone for help. It was really weird and strange in her house. As soon as I went through their front door, it was dark because the walls were painted dark blue and there were pornographic magazine cutouts all over their living room wall. My mother was never comfortable with us playing with Kunta Kentay over at her place, maybe because of that, but was always welcomed to come play with us at our house. Even though I wasn't able to go over to her house, I thought I'd go over there this particular day because we had no phone at the time and they were the only people we knew that lived close; it was an emergency. Her mom answered the door, so I asked my friend's mother to call 911 for my mom and tell them that she is really sick.

Kunta Kentay's mother asked me if I wanted to come in to use the phone, but I was too scared to go to their house. So I asked her if she could just bring the phone to me at the door because I was scared to go in. I couldn't help but notice the doorway walls and ceiling. As she was going to get the phone, I saw that they added pornographic cutouts on their doorway too! I kept thinking to myself as I was looking at the photos, *Oh my gosh! Look at all of these titties and booties everywhere! It's so nasty in here!* So Kunta's mother went to get her phone, bring it to me, and dialed the numbers for me. I told the emergency operator everything that was going on with my mother, and they assured me that someone was on their way to help. Then I went back home to let my mother know help was coming, and in the meantime, we just kept giving her cold towels and trying to give her ice-cold water to drink because she always liked icy cold water. When the paramedics arrived, they noticed the fear on a five-year-old girl's face, and all our faces and one of them said, "It's all right, y'all! Stop crying! Guess what? Your mother is going to be okay because she is just getting ready to have your baby brother!"

A Normal Childhood Fight

Sometimes in life, people whom you consider friends can become your worst enemies. Friends that turn foes are usually the worst because a good friend is hard to fight. I had my first childhood fight in kindergarten with a person whom I considered my first school friend. Not to mention, this particular friend was twice my size and the biggest kid in the class because she was bigger than your average kindergartener. I met my first school friend Rhoda in kindergarten at Hoover Elementary School in West Oakland, California. We were in the same classroom, and we sat at the same table directly across from one another. We became friends at the beginning of the school year because we always did our drawings together, talked to each other in class, and ate lunch together. During the beginning of that school year, while we became good friends, she started to tell me what to do and boss me around. I was her friend, so at first I didn't think anything of it and did what she wanted me to do.

One day, she wanted me to wear a blue rubber band on our hands as friendship bracelets, I did, but after a while, the rubber bands started making my hands numb and cold. I didn't like the way it felt, so I removed the so-called friendship bracelets, and she then yelled at me for doing so! She yelled, "You betta put those back on or you ain't gonna be my friend no mo!" I told her no, that the rubber bands hurt, and that I wasn't going to wear them. That must've rubbed her the wrong way, and after that, she rolled her eyes at me and said with a mean voice, "You're not my friend anymore then!" My response back to her was, "So what! I don't care!" and rolled my eyes back at her.

After that, we were both in trouble by the teacher because she overheard the commotion and put us both on timeout by facing the wall. The classroom laughed at us. After that incident happened between us, we were still friends, but she started bossing me around and would sometimes shove me, telling me to hurry up and walk faster when we were in line to go into class. Sometimes when she would shove me, I would trip over my foot, and some of the kids in line would laugh at me. I was sort of afraid of her because of her size, and I knew she would beat me up if I were to retaliate back. So I guess she was my bully-friend. One of the things she did that bothered me the most besides that was she would force me to sit down and allow her to play with my hair at lunchtime. We would be at the monkey bars, and she would play around with my long, thick hair and give me the most ridiculous hairstyle possible. After about the fourth time of me going to school with my hair done and getting back home with it looking like a wreck, the problem became too apparent.

My mother used to question me about my hair when I'd get home from school, and every time I just told her that I did it. On one occasion, my bangs ended up having to get cut because Rhoda made a whole patch in the front of my head with these tiny single-hair knots. That's when I told the truth about the hairstyles that Rhoda was doing to my hair. My older sister got mad at me and told me to tell the girl to stay out of my hair, and that's when my mother wrote a note to the teacher to make sure the girl would no longer play with my hair during lunchtime. The teacher followed up with my mother's note and instructed the girl to stay out of my hair. Sure enough, when lunchtime came, the girl approached me and told me to follow her over to the monkey bars so she could do my hair. I stood up for myself and told her no, which elevated her aggression toward me and made her want to fight in secret. I was so surprised that she didn't say anything to me at the time, but she did in fact leave me alone. She left me alone back in class too which was odd and strange because I've never seen her so quiet! I felt that me finally putting my foot down to her really worked, but on my way home to leave to the school gate to meet with my sister, she came up from behind me and attacked. She yanked my ponytail and started saying mean things to me about my hair, saying that it's nappy, dirty, and that she should just pull it out of my head!

I didn't know how to respond because I thought she was my friend and she understood her boundaries. I cried and was scared because we were in the schoolyard. I felt so helpless at that moment because kids were running around, playing, and screaming, so no one was really able to notice what was happening! Then when she let go of my hair, she said, "I should mess up your face!"

I cried, "I'm going to tell!"

She then scratched up my face and ran out of the school gate away from me. I was upset and mad because I thought she was my friend and that we were cool with each other. I was left walking to the gate confused.

It didn't matter how I felt about the relationship anymore because she attacked me first and scratched up my entire face. My skin was burning and stinging as I was walking toward the gate, crying, and of course, the salt from my tears didn't make the pain any better. I should have fought back but was scared and too stupid to realize that she never was really my friend in the first place. After my sister and I got home, I just went on my regular day and to get ready to eat and do my homework. When my older sister got home from school, she saw my face and got so upset!

She said with a mad tone, "Willa, what happened to you? Who did that to your face?"

I replied, "Did what?"

She made me get up from my seat, took me to our bathroom to make me look in the mirror at the damage on my face. She said, "This!" as she pointed toward my face. I felt compelled to tell my sister what had happened because after looking at what Rhoda did to my face, I was now mad and sad at the same time! My older sister was so heated and angry that with my mother's approval, she left her class early the next day to meet me at the gate where the kindergartners hung out to wait for their guardians or parents to meet them after school. She had me show her the way Rhoda walked to leave out of the gate. So to our surprise, she actually walked home by herself.

Once we met up to her, she realized I was with a girl her size, just a little taller, and realized what was about to happen after my sister exchanged words to her about what she did to me. I noticed that she looked a little scared of my sister because she knew she was no match for my oldest sister! My sister didn't have to use any force because of the fear she pumped inside of Rhoda, and it showed through her facial expression, and she promised not to mess with me anymore. That made me so happy to see how afraid she was of my sister. This really opened up my eyes to what was going on with this girl.

My sister said, "No wonder that girl was messing with your hair and messed up your face like that! Her hair is two inches long and she's ugly."

We laughed aloud as we walked away, and Rhoda never bothered me again in class or on the yard. That was the first time I learned about jealousy and fake friendships. I was a little traumatized because I was six years old and realized that even if you try to be nice to someone, they could still hate you because you look better than them.

Now that Bill is gone, school's out for the summer, and we didn't have to be locked in the room anymore, my mother allowed us to have friends over. I ended up with a friend whose mother was a nurse who lived around the corner from us and another friend who lived in the same duplex as they did. We were all good friends, and they would usually come over at the same time to visit. We always played board games and dolls.

One day, we were all playing in my room and decided to play dolls, the grown-up version, for whatever reason. Of course at the time, I didn't think these incidents I'm about to describe were weird, but reflecting back, I don't know what in the world conspired us to do the unthinkable. What we were thinking is beyond what kids our ages should've been thinking.

At first, our doll play was innocent, and we were just girls having fun playing with friends. Somehow on this particular day, while we were playing, we started making the dolls have sex with each other. Well, of course two dolls can't have intercourse, but we rubbed the dolls together where their private parts would be, trying to make them have sex. We laughed and giggled while rubbing the dolls together and making sounds. We were doing things with the dolls that I saw grown-ups do in the movies. Then things got even weirder when we all got aroused from what we were doing that we wanted to try the real thing.

We all decided to try what we were doing with the dolls on each other, so we went into the closet together and closed the door so that no one would see what we were doing. We then began touching each other as we did on the dolls. Without no one knowing what we were doing, we continued what we were doing until we thought someone was coming. It was strange because we played with our toys afterwards as if nothing happened! We made a vow to never tell no one about what we did so that we wouldn't get in trouble. And that we did. The next time they came over to play, we didn't talk about what happened on the previous visit. We played with our dolls the same way we did before, but this time, we didn't go into the closet, and then we went to the backyard to play outside. We didn't do the closet again; however, when we played with our dolls, it was not always childlike.

Moving into Big Momma's House

My big momma was an amazing woman who incredibly bore thirteen children, seven boys and six girls, and my mother was the oldest of the bunch. I always admired her for having so many children. My grandmother's doors were always open to her children, no matter how crowded the house would get. Somehow, her children and grandchildren managed to fit in her four-bedroom and two-bathroom house. Big Momma's house also included two living rooms (one upstairs and one downstairs), one den that we called the breakfast room that had a stairway that leads downstairs, a small washroom, two hallway closets, a tiny backyard stairs porch, a front yard porch, two driveways, one that led to the garage and one that was alongside the house that could easily park three cars.

The house was a two-story house with a lot of floor space. When we moved back to Granny's house, I was still seven years old and not ready for this new overcrowded lifestyle. Being cramped up with my sisters and brother was one thing and not really uncomfortable because we were a family of six. On the other hand, what choice did we have but to be sardined in with other relatives or be homeless with no roof over our heads. So Big Momma's house was my mother's only affordable emergency plan.

Everybody in the neighborhood knew Big Momma's house on Ninety-Sixth and Plymouth Street. That particular house was the neighborhood's entertainment house known for something dramatic always taking place. It was most definitely crowded in the home. Big Momma's home was a residence for my mother (who was the oldest of the thirteen of my grandmother's children), her five children, my auntie the (second oldest) who had four children all boys, one of my uncles who had one child, a son; my other aunties and uncles who were living there when we moved back in, had no children. In total, there were twenty-three people living in this two-story, four-bed-room house, trying to make the space work.

The space limitations were usually a constant issue and almost an everyday battle. There were constant family clashes taking place inside the house and outside the house. The family clashes were toxic, violent, and mostly fueled from drugs and alcohol. Growing up in this house made for many crazy memories that are hard to forget. There was always a dramatic or violent episode of some sort happening, whether it was about food, clothes, money, personal items, or invasion of space! One of my uncles seemed to be really envious of my mother and her son. He was constantly comparing his only son to my mother's only son which was my baby brother. What he used to do was give my mother a hard time by making my siblings and I clean up behind all twenty-three (including ourselves) people in the house. We literally had to do whatever we were told in the house without question. The boys in the home (which were my auntie's boys) were never given chores or any task to do.

The other children in the house were my auntie's four sons who had a father who would frequently check on the boys from time to time. Their dad used to make sure that my uncle didn't take advantage or mistreat them in any way because he knew how my uncle was. Also, my uncle's son didn't have to lift one finger or help with anything in the house. This just left me and my sisters to take on all house chores, excluding my brother because he was too small to be used for any housework at that time. Once again, my mother was back on drugs because she was so vulnerable to my uncle and his bullying ways, especially because we didn't have a dad like my cousins to defend us from his mistreatment. I understood that it was important for us to have chores to teach us responsibility and that children should help their parents out, but on the contrary, we took on all the chores, and it was tough cleaning after so many people at the age of seven years old. It was tough and hard because I was still learning how to wash dishes. I always hated being interrupted from playing outside with my friends to fix someone a glass of ice water or to get the remote controller that was clearly in arms reach of the aunt or uncle who made those types of requests.

Our chore duties included washing clothes, drying clothes, cleaning the bathroom, cleaning out the attic, cleaning the kitchen, sweeping all the floors, cleaning out all the closets, picking clothes up off the floor, cleaning the front yard, backyard, and porch, cleaning the refrigerator, and sometimes making our own food (which was the fun chore). Taking out the trash and making store runs weren't so bad because sometimes we'd get a treat or fifty cents to a dollar for it. On the contrary, some of these tasks didn't seem so bad, but multiplying these duties by twenty-four people and the work for a seven-year-old was way too much.

Washing clothes wasn't too bad if the washer wasn't broken, but the times when the washer wasn't functioning properly, that was a nightmare. We had to wash the clothes by hand in the tub or suffer the embarrassment of fitting as many clothes as possible in a grocery cart, and then pushing the cart down Cherry Street to the Birch Street laundromat. Even though washing clothes in the tub was a harder task than going to the laundromat, I still preferred using the tub. The walk past Cherry Street to the laundromat was my stumbling block because of the neighborhood bullies. It was frustrating because I could've taken a different route to the wash house, but that route was a main street and a junior high school was located on that street and I was too embarrassed to walk that way with a bunch of clothes.

Whenever the coast was clear to walk to that particular laundromat, the experience wasn't so bad at all for me because I sometimes received one dollar and fifty cents for the task, and the lady who owned the laundromat had a small room there that was her candy store. She had a few arcade machines there, and she was always so sweet and nice. She sold ice cream cones for fifty cents and twenty fifty-cent candy bars. So I'd use one dollar for an ice cream, candy, and fifty cents for the arcade machine, which was twenty-five cents per game. Pacman was my favorite game to play.

They would violate me anyway possible: they would yell out sexual slurs, grab my private parts, and they would hold me tight and hump on my butt, then shoo me away like I was nothing. We never had a dryer, so depending on the house finances, we would endure Cherry Street or just hang the clothes up on a clothesline in the backyard.

One of the worst duties was cleaning the bathrooms because when the toilet tissue ran out, people would just use clothes to wipe their butts. The bathroom would get so disgusting, shirts, pants, socks, underwear, whatever clothes that were thrown behind the bathroom door that were used after when people did the number two to wipe their butts. I did my best not to throw up from the look and the smell of all those stinky clothes. It got to the point where I felt like it was a luxury to be able to wipe myself with newspaper or the pages from a book when we ran out of tissue. I remember going through the clothes behind the door, shaking off the roaches and the spiders, looking for an unused poop or pee spot on the clothes to wipe myself after using the toilet.

The next cleaning assignment that I hated to do was the attic and the garage. Now, we didn't have to clean the attic but once. I remember it being very dark, scary, and full of spiderwebs. My uncle showed me how to access it from the kitchen, as if it was no big deal. I guess the attic wasn't a priority or my uncle noticed how terrified I was 'cause I only remember having to go up there once. There was no such luck when it came to the garage, and every few months, we had to do the insurmountable task of cleaning out the garage.

The garage was a hazardous place that no one really wanted to go in. It was basically used for dumping unwanted or old outdated items that were once in the house. Whenever the garage was filled to capacity, my sisters and I would then remove as much as possible out to the street for pickup. That stuff was such a waste, I don't even think passersby or dumpster divers wanted any of it. I just would be shocked if any of our junk ended up being anybody else's treasure.

It was not a house always stocked with food, so I used to scratch my head trying to figure out why the refrigerator was so gross. Thinking back, I know that the refrigerator had to be crawling with salmonella and a whole bunch of other bacterial diseases, and it amazes me that we were never really sick a lot. I don't know what kind of refrigerator it was because it only had one shelf, and whatever food that was in there was just cramped and stacked on top of each other. I hated removing all the spoiled, moldy food that was mixed in with the food that was supposed to be edible. I guess the reason why we didn't really get sick of the food is because the leftover food in the refrigerator was off-limits to my sisters and I anyway. I don't think we would have eaten that leftover food even if we could. Some days, I dug through it and got lucky to find something edible.

We actually learned to be real creative with what we knew was fresh. Somehow, we always had potatoes, and one of my uncles worked at the Salvation Army, so he would bring home free bread and cheese. My common food diet was potatoes, bread, and cheese. I ate cheese toast, cinnamon toast, syrup toast, mayonnaise sandwiches, and French fries. We always had cereal and Top Ramen on hand for the most part. Sometimes we had fried bologna with Lay's potato chips and 7UP soda pop, which seemed like a special occasion. Big Momma did make everyone a three-course homemade dinner every Sunday, which always reminded me that there was always that one day out of the week that we'd have a delicious home-cooked meal that she prepared, and on holidays, it was the best food ever!

When it came to food, it was just kinda like every man for himself most of the time. Even my aunts and uncles would argue among each other about if someone ate their leftover or saved food.

The other duty I had that was actually like a treat was when I was asked to make store runs. If I got the chance to go to the store for one of my aunts or uncles, they would actually be kind enough to pay fifty cents up to a whole dollar. That was a lot of money to a kid back then. With my twenty-five cents, I could get one pack of sunflower seeds, penny candies, a box of Boston baked beans, a small pack of chips, or a quarter juice. The highest reward for a store run was one full dollar, which for me at that age was like hitting the jackpot. One dollar actually meant I could get some meat, like a fifty-cent pack of dry salami, a small bag of chips, one pack of Now and Laters, a box of Boston baked beans, and a five-cent gum. Made for a really cool snack! I really didn't complain about making store runs because honestly, the store runs were one of the best things about doing out-of-the-home errands at those times.

Welcome Back, Daddy

Days turned into weeks, months went into a full year, and just about the time I was eight years old, I was used to the systematic routine of my everyday lifestyle. I was starting to miss my daddy, and I prayed so hard to God that he would bring him to come see me. I always yearned for a father figure, something that I truly longed for. Even though I knew that he was too crazy for my mommy, I still missed him. Weeks went by, then boom, out of nowhere, I started getting random weekly visits from my father. That always gave me hope that having a father around would spark some limitations on what was required of his children in that house and that maybe some of the things going on would change. Sometimes he would take me and my sisters to the park on the sunny side to get free lunch. This was great because not only did I get to spend time with my daddy, but I got to also eat a nutritious fun meal that felt like I was on a lunch date with my daddy. It was so much fun hanging out with him because I always felt like I was his favorite, and his kisses and hugs were always what I longed for.

From time to time, our visits always took place at our grandmother's house on my dad's side of the family. My grandmother conveniently lived several short blocks away from Big Momma's house on Ninety-Fourth and Hillside. Her home was nestled in the back unit of a duplex with a beautiful big flower bush by her porch. Her small one-bedroom home was so quiet and cozy. Her bathroom always used to smell like Irish Spring or Coast soap, and her kitchen smelled like Palmolive dishwashing liquid. I loved spending the nights with her and sleeping on her cozy pull-out couch. I was so looking forward to things turning around with these new visits by my father. It didn't bother me if my dad and mom didn't get back together. I knew that he was physically abusive as well as a bad drug influence, and I wanted my mother to be safe from him. However, my heart had me feeling that maybe if my father had given up on drugs, just maybe, he would get his own place and get himself back together. I was so mad at him in a sense because I couldn't dream of him getting back together with my mother but still loved him so much and wanted to have him around as my father at all times. Unfortunately, after a while, the visits didn't become permanent like I longed for, and I was left with a confusing yet heartbroken visit with my father after our last particular visit.

My First Five Dollars

My grandmother always dressed us up really fancy and pressed our hair when it would be holiday visits when my dad took us to visit with her. She even made us dresses to wear. She used to make all sorts of handcrafted items that she used to sell at her local senior citizens organization. She used to make delicious homemade plum jellies, which she sold around the neighborhood and senior citizen center. People loved her plum jellies; they were a favorite especially in her neighborhood. She grew her own plum trees in her backyard and used her plums to make the jelly with. I was always curious about her jams, and I asked her what all the jelly jars were for, not realizing her entrepreneur spirit. My hand would even get spanked if I touched too many display plum jars on her kitchen shelf. I never realized the value of those delicious plum jellies and took to heart a sneaking chance to taste some. Even though I was only eight years old and it seemed like something the much older folks indulged in, the plum jelly quickly became my favorite after she let me taste it. My grandmother used to have family gatherings at least one to two times a year where family from outside and inside of California would come to visit.

On this last pick-up visit from my father, he decided he would take my sisters and I to see our older cousins that flew in from down south at our grandmother's house. So while we were there for the visit, I really had a great time. We got to spend time with our cousins that we hadn't seen in a while and play with them. My grandmother used to cook so much food. Her food was so delicious, and she baked really well too! My dad used to describe her food as "Boomin," meaning so really good and delicious. Another bonus to this visit that day was that my older cousin from down south gave me five dollars as a big surprise monetary gift. It was the first five dollars I ever had, and I felt so happy to have received such a big gift. That five dollars was the biggest money I ever had before. The reunion was great; I had so much fun with my dad's family and took so many photos. My grandmother even went out of her way that day to make us look really pretty by handknitting our dresses for us to wear and pressing our hair with ribbons and barrettes even though she had so much food to cook and have her place ready to entertain the company. Her hands were quite full that day. The dresses that she created for us for that family function reinforced the fact that this was meant to be a very special day.

After we changed back into our normal clothes, it was time to walk from my dad's mother's house, on Hillside in Ninety-Fourth, back home to my grandmother's house on Ninety-Sixth in Plymouth. I had the happiest walk I ever had with my dad and thinking so hard about how I was going to spend my first ever five dollars for the next day. The walk back home was actually relieving because for the first time in years, I was able to have a fun chat with my dad about his relatives. The walk felt very long, which was a good thing since I felt like I had a great father-and-daughter moment with my dad. Once we arrived at my other grandmother's house where we were staying, my father had this serious look on his face like something came over him. I noticed his face started sweating. So as he was ready to depart from our presence, he knelt to me and asked in a whispering tone "Where's your five dollars at?"

I quickly thought that he asked me this to make sure I didn't lose it during our walk back home. So I excitedly responded to my dad, "It's right here in my pocket!"

Then he said in a strong tone, "Give it to me!"

Now, the way he said it put fear in me because he's never asked me for anything before, especially not in that heavy tone. It was at that very moment that I knew he was serious about wanting my five dollars. I'm guessing he noticed my eyes watering up when I handed my money to him with sadness because he immediately told me to not ask questions about it. He quickly kissed me on my cheek and said, "Thank you and I love you. See you later!" and he left me.

The best way that I can describe the feeling that I felt at that moment was as if I swallowed my heart into my gut and then pooped it out! Not only was I hurt, mad, and sad, but I felt so empty and heartbroken. I couldn't even talk. I was speechless! I felt that my dad took something from me that I could finally call a jackpot and brag to my other cousins about. My dad had a struggle that at times I really didn't understand.

All Right, Daddy, One Last Visit for Now

Probably a month after my daddy stole my five dollars, he came back for what became his last visit. To put it more accurately, this visit was his last visit for a very long time. I'll admit that I was a "daddy's little girl," and it was hard for me not to forgive him and just want him to be my father again. I was long over that five dollars. I was just so happy to see him and excited that he wanted to take me to the park to get a free lunch again. I was really enjoying the time at the park with him, but I couldn't help but notice that he seemed sicker than the normal effects of the drug relapse. He was sweating a lot and actually appeared to be more different than his regular self.

As usual, after we left from playing at the neighborhood park, we walked back over to Big Momma's house where I was living. My grandmother was making some of her delicious stew that she made from scratch, and you could smell the aroma all through the block! My grandmother used to make the best homemade stew which was very healing for help with relieving bad colds. So he asked my grandmother to leave him the soup in the pot after she finished cooking the stew, which they called pot liquor. As my father gulped down all that liquid, I couldn't help shake the thought that he was really drinking a lot of leftover grease with the soup. Then he smiled and, in his silly tone of voice, said to me, "Now that's what you need to drink when you don't feel good!" Then we both laughed because I thought it was funny because it seemed gross to me. He was so happy, I was so happy, and once again, for what would be a long time in a while, we walked around the neighborhood to visit his friends, and that made our visit even more special.

The Battle of the Uncles

When my father came by to visit and then left me at Big Momma's house, he had to have believed that he was leaving me in a better place. To my dismay, some of my uncles who lived in the house were a similar version of my father. The similarities, specifically, had to do with drug abuse and the dramatic fights they had between each other. Thank God there were no camera phones back then; otherwise, their fights would be viral right now and yet embarrassing.

At first, their behavior was rational, and their drug use wasn't noticeable to me. I mean, I was eight, almost nine years old, so what the adults were doing in the house wasn't really a concern to me. But my two uncles did dress up on occasion with a nice button-up shirt and had perfect neat afros with some cool shades on when they decided to barbeque for the family. They were really handsome fellas on some days. So whenever they weren't crazy and fighting, they seemed normal to me. My job was to stay in a child's place, which is what I always tried to do, but the fights were too much of a show to ignore.

The arguments initially started out over items that came up missing in the house. Most of the stuff that got stolen belonged to other relatives who lived in the house. This meant that, technically, the blame could have been on anyone, but I guess the blame had been narrowed down. Now, with my two uncles left to point the finger at each other; the Battle of the Uncles would begin.

I wish I could say once a week, once a month, or once a year, my two uncles got into a fight. The truth of the matter is, it just felt like they got into a fight all the time. The shouting would start in the house, as they yelled to determine who was the alpha male. If one was not willing to submit to the other, then the hollering would lead to shoving, which always turned into a wrestling match. Once the wrestling started, then the real chaos began and the fight would end up outside on the front porch, the driveway, or even out in the middle of the street. It didn't matter what other people in the house had to do; my uncles just got ready to rumble! No matter what time of the day it was!

It was showtime one evening, in the afterschool hours, when my two uncles got into it. There were some people downstairs, in the designated "get high" area, who finally left. The guest leaving from downstairs meant that all the drugs had been smoked up, and there was no more. One of the uncles went upstairs asking for change so he could get a beer, which could have been true, but he also used that line around the house to get more money for drugs. When his attempt for money failed, he went back downstairs, and like tag-team wrestlers, my other uncle came up and tried a more bullying approach. Uncle number 2 would go around the house asking for change in a more threatening way; he demanded other relatives in the house to help with some change through intimidation.

It was as if he forgot that he was asking for change from his siblings and would insinuate ridiculous consequences for those who wouldn't cooperate. After both uncles tried their good cop, bad cop tactics to persuade others in the house for money, they would have a meeting downstairs. It was like a plot. So after a little past an hour, I started hearing my two uncles bickering. This indicated that their feen for more crack had really kicked in, but they didn't have enough for more drugs. The crackling sound of the wooden stairs was my alarm clock that trouble was coming. If the sound was creepy, then that meant one of them would give another go at panhandling, but if the sound was loud stomps like the whole staircase was about to collapse, then it was showtime!

Sure enough, my two uncles had decided that since they couldn't get any more drugs or beer, then they knew someone or everybody in the house wasn't going to have any peace. Like two toddlers feeling ignored and neglected, my two uncles were now in the front room fussing at each other. These two grown toddlers even had their own language, which made it hard to know exactly what they were talking about. See, they had a way of arguing which was in a code that we didn't understand, but I'm sure their guest who left earlier could interpret. They'd say sentences to each other like, "You know what I'm talking about," "You know what the f—— it is," or "You better get outta my face with all that." They'd never say exactly what they were talking about or what specifically "it" is.

After they got tired of speaking in code back and forth, they finally instigated each other enough for their battle royal. The noise got louder and louder, and things in the house started to get knocked all over the place. My other uncles who lived in the house had seen and heard enough, so they pushed them outside. No one cared to break up the fiasco; getting them out of the house was just a way to deter their elevated chaos. One of the uncles hopped past the front porch and ran out to the middle of the street. Then he called the other out to continue the spectacle; he said, "Come on and meet me in my office."

Once both of the two uncles were "at the office" in the middle of the street, they started their intimidating taunting contest. It was like watching a kung fu mime versus a renaissance warrior swaying back and forth, except they added words. Each would say a phrase before his "macho, macho man" move. Uncle number 1 said, "Yeah, boy, it's full force, baby," then he squatted in a terrible sumo wrestler stance with his hands on his knees and rocked left to right. Uncle number 2 said, "You ain't s——," including a bunch of other vulgar words as he pranced around on his tippy toes in his own circle, pointing at his chest. Uncle number 2 kept his arms spread out during his performance as if to make himself wider or bigger.

The Crack Attack

My grandmother's youngest daughter who was only a few years older than my sister had a comical way of referring to her older brothers' performance. As everyone else in the house was ashamed as my two uncles embarrassed the family by entertaining everyone else on the block with their foolery, she came out to the porch, shaking her head with her hands on her hips, and said, "They must be having another crack attack again." Relatives who lived in the house had grown tired of the outside scene and had threatened the uncles that they would call the police. It was an attempt to get them to calm down 'cause, in reality, no one would ever call the cops. Maybe the idea of the local law enforcement was a helping remedy, at least it seemed that way. The two uncles must have needed to go through all this drama in order to wind down and release their frustration because that's as far as their fighting went this time.

Luckily, my two uncles could disperse without making contact with each other and get back into the house. One uncle went back downstairs by using the lower level side entrance to the house. The other uncle went through the front door and back into the front room. He assured the family that the movie was over and that he and his brother had no more crumbs to pick for the day. That was about as much reassurance as anyone in the house could hope for because like normal, this episode would be continued. There was nothing else to disturb me after this recurring event, so I took my eight-year-old self outside to play.

The Intruder Wants to Protect but Not This Time

Like I stated earlier, there were twenty-four people living in Big Momma's house, and ten of them were second-generation children. Out of the children, three of them had extra protection because their dad, who luckily for them, often came by to set the record straight. Now, normally, my cousin's dad would stop by and be a cordial visitor but, at the same time, command presence and respect. My uncles would hate it when he would stop by. I'd overhear them saying phrases like, "Dame, such and such is here." Of course, all the kids would love when "such and such" showed up. We'd all run up to him and say hi, and then with his deep voice, he'd say, "Hay, hay, hay, hay!"

He'd pat me on the head as a form of acknowledgment. Then his eyes would weed out all the children to locate his three boys. He was an alpha male, and all the adults in the house adhered to his concerns. If the adults were watching TV programs, those got ignored, and whatever mischief that was visible got put on hold. The front room would even become his barber shop. In his bag was all the tools needed to fully groom his boys.

He would cut my cousin's hair, give them some money, and give them clothes and shoes for school. He had a way of respectively indirectly getting his point across, and everyone knew that his visits were a routine checkup to make sure his boys were okay. It was like a social worker was stopping by, and everyone was on their best behavior because he wanted to make sure his sons weren't being mistreated and not to cross that line. I would stand around in admiration and wish that my cousins were my brothers and their father was my dad. Everything within me just couldn't stop yearning for that type of protection that his presence afforded his children.

The Intruder

D ave Chappell said it best in one of his comedy sketches, "Sometimes keeping it real goes wrong!" There was arguing on the steps of my grandmother's porch by the window where I was about to lie down on the floor to sleep. The voices got louder, then all of a sudden, I could tell that there were more than just two voices. It became clear that all six of my uncles were united and yelling at one person. I guess the size of the defending group didn't pose enough prevention 'cause next thing I knew, the arguing turned to rumbling. There was banging against the wall and the glass window next to where I was lying began to shake.

I ran to the front room and gathered there were other relatives in the house, and I got a clearer view of what was taking place on the porch. As I peered through the front room window, I couldn't believe who this other person was. The trespasser was the one who I always knew to be as a calm self-controlled alpha male: my three cousins' dad. Unlike the usual charades I commonly saw between my two uncles, this was a real full-on violent fight! No taunting or causing a scene for attention but a true scare of sorts. I watched in confusion and did not understand whose side to take.

There were right punches, left punches, and body slams all over the porch banister. My three cousins' dad was big, tall, and always appeared to be strong, but in this fight, he was betraying some Incredible Hulk-type of strength. He'd go to pouncing on one of my uncles and the other uncles would go to beating him in self-defense. At one point, they'd manage to get him off one of the uncles just to have to fend him off another. My cousin's father was so extremely strong that night that no one understood where his strength was coming from! It had to be a very dangerous situation for my uncles because it took six men to try and get my uncle-in-law to back away and leave the premises, but that just made him all the more crazier and stronger somehow. I overheard an adult say, "Maybe he must be on PCP and that's where his strength and craziness is coming from," and "I hope they get him to leave!"

When I heard the adult (not sure who it was who said it) say that, I was all the more afraid and was hoping the cops were coming. Initially, they had already called the cops, but by it being Oakland, California, the cops were more than likely busy with other criminal and violent activities. I believe that's why my uncles took matters into their own hands, and this was the first time I witnessed all my uncles coming together to make the house safe from harm. I heard my uncles plotting against the intruder, saying things to each other like, "You go get the bat from downstairs!" and "You go get the two-by-four board from the backyard!" So then I witnessed certain uncles leaving the fight to go get those items to use to help combat the uncle-in-law who had now been obviously under the influence of a strong narcotic and considered very dangerous.

When the two uncles left the fight, I heard a loud crashing sound that came from my grandmother's bedroom! We ran to go see what it was, and sure enough, a brick was thrown through her window! I heard my uncles (who had left to get the weapons) rushing back to the scene, screaming out loud, "Oh, hell no, did he just break Mommy's window?" and the others yelling back, "Yeah, he did, hurry up with the bat, we need the bat!"

So as I was standing there watching all this madness, I saw my uncles beating the intruder with the boards and bats. He was getting busted in the head. I saw the board land a serious direct hit to his legs behind the knees. Now with him (the intruder) sort of broken down to the ground, all six uncles were now on top of him, trying to pin him down, but he still managed to break loose, and he was still throwing serious punches toward my uncles.

Now that my uncle-in-law realized that they were doing everything in their power to contain him, he started to run down the street, and the chase began because now, at this point, my uncles were furious over the broken window, and they felt he might come back with a gun next. Now, the fight had made its way back in front of my grandmother's house, and everyone had blood on them, I believe to be coming from my uncle-in-law, and now it looked as if my uncles had finally worn the intruder down. I saw him panting, gasping for air, and throwing in the towel as he started to head out toward where he lived. This fight continued from night to early dawn, and the police never showed up, and just like in the movies, the police showed up when it was all over! I'm not sure what transpired this battle or why they tried to detain him, but it seemed as if my uncles were trying to keep him from coming into our home and were holding him down until the police arrived. Still, to this day, I never knew what that quarrel was really about, but it was scary.

Eight and Not so Great

Life had taken a different turn for me once I was now a mature eight-and-a-half-year-old kid. At that point in my life, I was able to walk to school by myself (which was about five long blocks to walk), make store runs, do chores that were given me, prepared and cooked food (whatever was available) without causing no problems, and doing as I was told. Life seemed to be on the up and up at this point as I was a kid who grew up in the hood, so whatever I was given or not given, I didn't complain at all.

My sisters and I always made the most out of our childhood. I especially loved playing with my friends who were mostly the neighborhood kids. One thing that I did admire the most about my childhood is when the grown-ups in the house never confined us and we were always able to play with our friends outside or at their houses; as long as my chores were done, I was free to roam the neighborhood. Maybe that wasn't a good idea, being I was just a little kid and all, but I did display a lot of maturity at my age. I was never in any kind of trouble at this point in my childhood; I always worked hard to get good grades in school because it made me feel good about myself when I used to receive my report that had all *Es* and *Gs*. We used to have a nickname for the really bad kids in the neighborhood; we used to call them "bey's kids" (like the kids in that cartoon) and a lot of those bey's bey's kids were my friends. Who knows those same kids probably considered us bey's bey's kids that lived in my grandmother's house in Ninety-Sixth on Plymouth Street because of the way it was. I was more of a tomboy at this age too, because I was always climbing trees and gates, playing baseball with the neighborhood boys, and trying to always find boards and nails in my grandmother's backyard to build things. I had my girly moments too when I'd hung out with my girlfriends and we'd play double Dutch, Chinese jump rope, and do cheer dances and games.

So on one of these days, as I'm outside across the street playing jump rope with my girlfriends, showing off my double Dutch skills (as it was my turn), my oldest boy cousin called my name aloud in a strange way. He was calling my name as if I needed to hurry up to see what he wanted because it seemed extremely important. Now this boy cousin of mine is the oldest son of my aunt who has four sons. Three of the younger sons are only by the same man who was the protector dad that I mentioned before whom I wished was my dad.

Not to give an excuse for the story I'm about to describe in regard to my older cousin, but decisions made out of his control may have contributed to his actions. His mother, my aunt, fell in love with a man from the south. It may have been a one-night stand or a long-lasting relationship, but the results ended up with my aunt getting pregnant. Come to find out this love affair was incest because that man she chose to lay down with was her very own cousin. In other words, my oldest cousin's father is also his second or third cousin. Maybe my aunt justified the relationship or whatever it was because he was a distant relative. It just seems like her actions cursed her son and tainted him with that same way of thinking. With all that said, I can get back to why when I was eight, it wasn't so great.

Back to when my oldest cousin called me up into the house, he made it seem as if it were like an emergency. When I got into the house, he started whispering from a hiding spot, gesturing with his two fingers for me to come here. He whispered, "Willia, Willia, come here." He didn't call me the correct spelling of my name which is Willa. When I got close enough to hear what he was saying, he then said, "Hey, go in Mommy's room," which is what we called Grandma. I thought something was weird about the way he was saying what he was saying, but I thought maybe we were going to play a prank on someone or something; however, I just didn't feel right as I walked down the hall to Momma's room. He wasn't in the room when I got in there. I just happened to look back and notice him looking the other way out of the hallway bathroom.

Once I got completely in the room, he told me to close the door all the way. After I closed the door, I felt like the world stopped; even though other kids were playing outside, I felt a numb silence. Shortly after I entered the room, my cousin came into the room and closed the door behind him. He then pushed the heavy dresser over in front of the door so it couldn't be easily opened. He then walked closer to me and kept saying shh, but the thing was that I wasn't even talking. Then he told me to lie down on my mommy's (Big Momma's) bed, but I was thinking he wanted me to lie down and go to sleep.

So when I laid down on my stomach, he then turned me around on my back and pulled down my pants. Once he got my pants off, he then took off my panties, and he put his mouth on my private part. After he would pause from what he was doing to me, he would stop and ask me if I liked it. At first, I just asked him to please stop because I was numb and I was in so much shock I couldn't believe this was happening. I couldn't even feel him down there because I was numb and started crying. I kept my hands over my eyes and just was crying, but he still kept asking me if I liked it. I hated the world, and I didn't want to see anything but darkness from my closed eyelids. Once I could speak a little, I started asking him to please just let me go back to play outside. I was so scared, mad, and ashamed. I couldn't believe what was going on, and it felt like forever.

It seemed like at least an hour went by until one of my uncles forced open the door a little. I thought I was saved when my uncle saw me, but he just acted like he didn't see it, as if he accidentally walked into the wrong room or something. I heard him say in a mean voice, "I need to come in there, and you need to come out!" My uncle then closed the door back and walked away. I guess that was his way of giving my cousin the cue that he should stop doing whatever it was he was doing. Then my cousin started touching himself, and I heard a quiet moan; he then collapsed on top of me. A few seconds later, he shook my leg, and I assumed it meant I could get up and go, and he said as I was putting myself back together, "Hey, don't tell nobody and wipe your face!"

When I left the room, I didn't have it in me to go back outside and pretend like everything was normal to anyone I walked past. I couldn't face the world at that moment, so I ran to the bathroom, sat on the toilet, and cried. I wept to get the "I can't believe what just happened to me" feeling out of my system so I could go back outside and finish playing jump rope as if nothing ever happened. I guess because I was so embarrassed by what had happened, I didn't want to show any signs of what had happened to me to my friends. When I returned back outside to finish playing with my friends, it felt like the whole world was staring at me. I felt so ashamed and yucky. I hated living at that moment but decided to just play with my friends to try and not think about it.

My cousin was the type of person in the hood that was considered a D-boy (dope dealer); that's what we used to call men in the hood where you can get your weed, crack, heroin, hop, etc. I think he was affiliated with a known gang called Cumi that didn't take any mess when it comes to their territory and their turf members. So in other words, my cousin was sort of looked up to in our home because my family felt a sense of security with him around to help ward off any intruders or any persons who may have caused a threat to our family; my cousin was the one to go to if any threats were to ever arise. If certain intruders knew he lived in my grandmother's house, then the word gets back out to not mess with anybody from that household or Cumi would come for you; that's how it was in the hood. So in other words, he was like a deterrent of some sort, like a pit bull, Rottweiler, or German shepherd in a yard, which gives an intruder a second thought of breaking and entering.

Even though I had an uncle who also was a protector of the family, he lived elsewhere with his own family. Since he had his own place and didn't stay there, if there happened to be any other threat, my older cousin would step in; he was that extra backup for the family. Unfortunately, in these types of neighborhoods, protection was always a good thing. In other words, there were threats posed to our family from time to time. For instance, other dope dealers in the neighborhood may have posed a threat because maybe one of my dope fiend uncles or aunties owed them some money.

This would cause fear that they would come and do something to them or my grandmother's house to recover their money to retaliate, an abusive or stalking boyfriend of any female in our household, or in the hood beef (fights among other neighbors or feuds) would randomly happen which made our household seem less vulnerable to these types of things that may occur. He was the go-to guy for troubles with any rivalry, but my uncle was much different than my cousin though. He worked an honest job and was starting a family of his own. He did things the right way; if someone or some people posed a threat to my grandmother, her children, or grandchildren, he would gather up his posse to fight for our family to ensure the safety of our family. This was the uncle that I mentioned earlier who had saved my mother from my dad's attack on my mother that almost cost her her life!

He was also very protective of the children in the family too! He would have never done such shameful things to me like that. I missed him staying there with us, so most times, as I got a little bit older, I would take up the opportunity to go stay at his house weeks at a time to get a break away from Big Momma's house. I had sleepless nights for about a week after what had happened between my cousin and me. I still didn't understand why he did that to me, and I started to question myself as a kid. Here I am, eight years old, and I thought what he did to me was my fault. I thought I may have triggered him to molest me due to the fact that I was a girl who jumped rope really well, or did I look too cute that day? I was all messed up, and I also thought it may have been my fault because I was mature for my age too.

I hung around girls that were a little older than me, so when I was eight, most of my friends were ages ten and up. After a couple of weeks passed, it felt really strange living with him in the same house. Every time I had to pass him up in the house, he was always friendly and nice to me; he always gave me a big smile that seemed so innocent as if nothing ever happened. I trusted the fact that maybe he didn't know what he did and didn't remember. So after, I stopped beating myself up and just hoped that was just something he was going through and he didn't know what he did so he wouldn't do it again. Wrong! I'll say maybe about a month later, I was given a chore to do by my grandmother which was to wash and hang up the washed clothes outside in the backyard on the clothing line.

So as I'm hanging the clothes up and thinking to myself which friend I wanted to go play with for that day after I get my chores done, I hear the back door opening in a screeching way. The back door to my grandmother's house was on the second floor of the house which had steps connected to it to walk down on to get to the backyard. So to my surprise, my cousin creeps down half the steps and does a whisper-yell to me, telling me to come here. I went to him thinking maybe he wanted to apologize to me about what had happened because he was just drunk or high or going through something and didn't mean to do it and he finally realized what he did. He told me to meet him in the bathroom when I was done. To me, I was thinking that secretly he wanted to apologize without anyone hearing his apology.

He was my cousin, and I truly loved him because we were a tight-knit family who loved each other even in our dysfunctions. I didn't hate him at that time. I just wanted to give him the benefit of doubt. When I was done hanging up the clothes, as I was walking through the kitchen to go to the living room to let my grandma know I was done, I noticed my cousin peeping out the bathroom door, and when he noticed I saw him, he said, "Hey!" I told him, "I'll be back. I'm telling Mommy I'm done with the clothes!"

He said, "Okay, hurry up!"

I was so determined to see what he wanted that I ran to the bathroom!

Once I went into the bathroom, I noticed he had a bottle of cooking grease in his hand, and he told me to lie on the floor.

I said, "Why do I have to lie on the floor? It's dirty."

He replied with an attitude, "Just do it and lie down!"

I didn't want to, and he saw that I was hesitant and started to cry.

He said, "I'll give you a quarter if you do."

I said, "No, I don't want no quarter. I just want to go outside and play with my friends."

He then picked me up, laid me down on the floor with a gentle force, and took my pants off. I started crying as he pulled down his pants, then he poured cooking oil on his hand and rubbed it on his private part and poured grease on my private. As I was crying, he kept telling me to be quiet, and he kept putting his hand over my mouth because my crying sounds were getting loud while rubbing his private part over my privates.

I was so angry, mad, and hurt. I felt so deceived and helpless. I was hoping so bad that somebody would just open the door and tell him to get off of me. Life apparently was continuing on the outside of the bathroom door as if nothing was happening in the bathroom. I kicked and cried loudly, but nobody came to my aid. The house was usually loud in the daytime, and with him holding his hand over my mouth, no one probably noticed. Maybe no one was in the house at that time. After my cousin ejaculated on my private, he stood me up and said, "See, that was fast! Why you trippin, Willia? You can go outside and play now, so stop crying, Willia."

He said it like it was completely normal what he just did to me and as if it would be my new norm and to just take it and move on. I was furiously upset, and when he left the bathroom, I was so mad and crying while cleaning his semen off of me. It had a strong smell to it, and it was yucky and gross. For a moment, I thought I was cleaning a grayish white smelly slime off of my body! I was so angry and numb all over again. I felt betrayed. I was looking forward to playing with my friends that day, but after my cousin violated me again, I hated everybody and just wanted to hide myself away from the world.

So now that I'm all shook up, I couldn't find it in my heart to go back outside, knock on my friend's door, look at her with a straight face, and ask her and her sister to come outside to play with me. I took my little ole mad self in my grandmother's room, tucked myself on the side of her bed, and took a nap. I had cried myself to sleep then was woken up to bring the dry clothes in the house. As the months were going by, I was at a point where I'm now having trust issues. I'm not just being this little simple kid anymore that's doing the norms as I used to. I used to do things like wake up early in the morning, go to school, come home, do chores, and possibly run an errand, then my homework, go outside to play, come in when it's dark outside, eat, bathe, and go to sleep. My systematic ways changed a whole lot different from that. Going to school wasn't my cup of tea anymore because of sleepless nights and stress. It was so hard to focus on school, homework, and chores. My mind sometimes wandered off to fairytale land somewhere. I couldn't think straight.

I used to be so scared at night because if the day went by and my cousin didn't hem me up for a licky or greasy private part time, I had that bad feeling that maybe he'd try and creep on me at night while I'm sleeping. I used to hide on the side of my grandmother's bed, thinking that if I wrap myself up in the blanket, he wouldn't notice me and by me being so wrapped up in the blanket, he wouldn't be able to untangle me so he'll not mess with me. So I was wrong in my thoughts again!

One day, everything was going great; my uncles went out and bought VHS movies and popcorn seeds to pop some good ol' home-made popcorn for the entire family for an in-house movie night. All the kids and adults, including myself, were very excited because my uncles brought some good movies that we've been longing to see.

The grown-ups took all the couch space and chairs, and all the kids gathered together on the floor like at a campfire, which we truly loved to do; popcorn gets popped and then viola! The movie finally begins! Oh, that was always a great treat for us all as a unit. Movie time was our best quality time moment, and everything just seemed so right! Eventually, everyone falls to sleep after the movies, and just like a normal household, some people have to get up for work the next day and the kids for school. So we all headed to our sleeping quarters. As for me, I liked laying on my grandmother's bed because sleeping in the same room and bed with her was comforting and soothing for me.

Now that it was time for me to go to bed, I admired how my day was going thus far, and I noticed that I didn't see my cousin that whole day. Then I remembered that sometimes he'd still come in the house late from possibly grinding all day. When that thought came into play, I wrapped myself like a burrito in my sheet and tucked far under the excess mattress on the bed that I slept on with my grand-mother and youngest aunt. It was like a little honeycomb hideout of some sort. So I was finally in a good sleep, then all of a sudden, I felt a hand patting around my body like it was searching for something. I laid so still that I even held my breath, hoping that what I realized was my cousin would've thought I was a pile of clothes or something. When his hand patted my feet then grabbed and felt my toes, he tried to shake me lightly and quietly to wake me up.

I played dead like a wounded human, still alive from a bear attack! He didn't give up, so he slid me down like I was on a slide on to the floor and dragged the tail of the sheet I was wrapped in out of my grandma's room, down the hall, then into the bathroom. I mean his crazy ass dragged me like a serial killer dragging a dead person's body to a ditch! How rude, desperate, and shameful of him! I was in a state of shock that my tear ducts were dry! Now that he had me in the bathroom (again), I'm so mad at my cousin that I actually kept telling him to leave me alone, and I begged and pleaded for him to let me go. He had some cooking oil with him (again) and did his thing again! But this time, it was a combination of him licking my privates, rubbing my chest, and putting his mouth there (I did not have a breast), and this time, I noticed he was drunk. I cried. He put his hand over my mouth and locked down on me, trying to put his greasy private into my private! I tried to bite the inside of his hand, but his palm wasn't close enough for me to grip.

That felt like a whole different level of what I was used to in our encounters. I couldn't, for the life of me, bite his hand to scream because of how his hand was over my mouth. I felt the more that I tried to fight, the longer he took, so I just gave in and let him have his way so it could be over with! It still took too long for him to finish, and I just dealt with it. I felt hopeless, like there was nothing I could do at this point but just hope the people in the house would kick him out or he'd just get caught from selling drugs or something. I knew the chances of that were unlikely, so I just tucked my chin up and became this person instead of a kid, because in my heart, I knew that normal kids didn't go through this in their own homes!

I then took a stand against myself and told my heart that this is only temporary until my mom gets her own place and I'll just pray to God for a miracle for us. I prayed to God to please put our family in our own home! I mean, what was a girl to do? All I could do was go out on faith and a prayer to the heavens. I never wanted to go to a foster home to be split apart from my sisters and my close cousins who were my best friends. Foster care was not an option. My heart wouldn't let me do it. As a matter of fact, us kids going to a foster home was so out of the question that once my grandmother and late grandfather's house had been seeming to fall apart. I mean roaches, rats, and daddy long leg spiders became permanent tenants. Clothes, I mean like thousands of clothes, everywhere, it had that whole feel as in today's times, you would say the inside of the house in some of the rooms looked like a hoarder's situation.

One day, mysteriously, a child protection worker popped up at our home! She came in the house and witnessed the living conditions of the home and requested the adults about fixing up the place. She assured the adults that when she comes back and the house isn't properly cleaned up, she was going to have all us kids from my grandmother's house removed immediately!

We kids overheard her tell the adults that, and when she left, questions were raised of who could've possibly called the people on us! I knew it had to be the people who resided right directly across the street from us because every time my uncles had their episodes, or any fiasco went down, they always had front center chairs watching every bit of the scene being carried out.

But back to the CPS worker, when we kids learned what was about to happen, we all gathered together and let all the grown-ups know that we were going to get the house cleaned up spick-and-span! We cried because of the thought of losing each other, and that's why we are all still close till this very day. Two of them are no longer with us but in the presence of God. That's why I didn't want to risk us all losing each other by telling someone out of the home because I knew of the damage it would have caused us kids! So I kept my lips sealed and held my water for the meantime.

Nine and Right in Time

The pain and disappointment I experienced while I was eight really helped strengthen me as I matured. It also triggered me to be not so good as a kid anymore as well. One can sort of say that the shame and embarrassment helped encouraged my hardcore and distrustful ways. I also picked up some sexual tendencies that I couldn't control, and I didn't understand why I was doing the things I was doing. Yes, I've cried about it a lot after I would commit shameful sexual acts. "What is wrong with me?" That was a question I asked myself all the time during this stage of being a nine-year-old kid. I always felt there was a dark cloud hovering over my head. I did not understand my whole purpose in life and felt like I was just simply existing. I later picked up more tomboyish ways. I didn't feel girly at this stage in my life because I no longer felt cute but tough and hard. I became interested in scientific things such as learning about bugs. Searching for bugs in the dirt areas in the backyard was very soothing and calming for me. I wasn't afraid to touch the insects that I would find, holding them in my hand. I became even more interested in finding salamanders and worms, ladybugs, and rollie pollies (pill bugs). Don't know what came over me, but I wanted to just look for bugs outside and put them in jars, then after observing them for a while I released them back in the dirt or grass. Eventually, that feeling of studying bugs faded away.

I then started playing with boys more than girls. I felt that maybe boys could understand me more and I understood them. Girls wanted to talk about other girls, fight, and things weren't the same anymore with my girl friends. Even though we were kids, girls at that time seemed way mature than their ages, including myself. I was confused at this age because I wasn't sure who I was or what I was. I didn't feel like I was a kid. Now that time has passed, I was finding myself playing with boys more than with girls. I was also more aggressive in my behavior toward boys than ever before. See, at first I used to be a scaredy-cat of my bullies, but at the age of nine, I started to find myself fighting back!

One time, as I was on my way to the store for my uncle, the two bullies (a.k.a. the Cherry Street kids) spotted me crossing the main street and ran to catch up with me. One of them said, "Aye, blackie! Give me a quarter?"

I said, "No! I ain't got no quarter!"

He replied back, "Yes, you do! I know you do, so stop lying and give me a quarter!"

Something came over me, and I didn't get scared like I used to. I stared him hard in his face, breathing heavy this time; I felt as if I wanted him to try something with me so I could have a reason to punch him in his face. Luckily for us both, he must've felt my vibes and energy because he switched his attitude and started portraying to be my friend.

He asked, "You going to school tomorrow?"

I said, "Yeah, why?

His cousin then looked at me and said, "If you see my brother, tell him we said hi!"

I said, "Who's your brother?"

They replied, "Don!"

I was shocked when they told me who their brother was because he was a good friend in my class and I had no idea that they were related. I said, "That's your brother? I know him! Okay, I will tell him hi for y'all! He's in my class!"

After I said that, they left. I was shocked and relieved because I would've hit him, and they both would've jumped me! I had a lot of anger stored up in me at this point. But I was so glad that everything had worked out with them. From that point, we became somewhat friends, and I became friends with Don and his girl cousins outside of the classroom.

Thanks, Pretty Girlfriend, for the Break

There were multiple incidents of my oldest cousin coming on to me and getting his pleasure. What I remember during the time when I was nine is when I actually got a break from all the molestation. The best feeling in the world at this day and in my life is when my cousin found love! The day when I realized he had a new girlfriend is when he brought home a young lady who he seemed really into. The day when I first met her, I saw them walking from the corner of Ninety-Eighth coming down our street, and as they were walking toward our home, I noticed that they were holding hands and smiling at each other while having what looked like a nice conversation. As they were approaching where I was playing, I couldn't help but to smile the biggest smile I ever had at that time. Not because I was happy that he found love, but because I saw a normal older boy cousin that's doing what normal males do at his age instead of dealing drugs and doing what he was doing to me. I felt actually happy for him because in my nine-year-old mind, I was thinking maybe what he needed all along was a girlfriend, someone he should love to have as a companion and sexual relationship with.

When they came up to me where I was playing, I looked to my cousin and said, "HI, cousin, who's this pretty lady?"

He said, "Hi, Willia, this Diane, my new girlfriend!" He said it with so much excitement that I could tell he was in love.

She then looked at me and said, "Hi, I like your hair!"

I felt like giving her a big hug when she said that because no one ever said that to me because I used to do all kinds of wacky hairdos to my hair. She had the most beautiful smile, and her eyes were extremely gorgeous; they were the color of a hazel shining gem. She had the cutest hairstyle; it was so on point you couldn't find a flaw on her.

I then looked to my cousin and said to him, "Cousin, your girlfriend is very pretty, and she is so nice!"

They both said thank you at the same time. As they were walking away to go inside the house, other relatives came out to see her and welcomed her with open arms and love.

That's one thing for sure I can say about my relatives is that I do admire the way they welcome and love everybody that they come into contact with. That moment felt so normal compared to what I was used to that I just knew that the storm waters were then calmed. I was in the best mood ever at this point that I left my friends that I were playing with to go inside and see what others were saying about her and to see if he was going to go somewhere private with her. I guess my main curiosity before getting my hopes all too high was, was he going to do the nasty with her? I questioned this to myself because I hoped that he would so it would keep him away from me if he is getting sexual pleasures from her. I mean, she was so beautiful that even some of my uncles wanted her when they saw her too, so why wouldn't he? Sure enough, he left from taking her around the house and introducing her to everybody to his secluded room that he had in the house. I was so overjoyed that I took my little nosey self back outside, finished playing with my friends, and even let my friends take my turn while playing Chinese jump rope! I was a happy little girl who felt like the weight of the world had finally been lifted off of my shoulders because I knew, once he took her in his private area, anything was bound to arise! "Yes!" is all I kept telling myself that day.

So after a while of them being in my cousin's little honeycomb hideout, they finally came walking down the stairs outside in our front yard. I stared at them so hard, trying to see if there was a difference in her walk, a look to their faces as if they did something nasty to each other, or even a change in body language. As I was still play-ing with friends, a couple of my siblings, and cousins, I whispered to the other kids, "Look how she is walking, they did the nasty, I can tell, can't y'all?" We started chuckling among each other and saying aloud, "Ooh, y'all did the nasty!" pointing at them as we told that to them. Then I said aloud to my cousin as they were a little ways down the block "Ooh, Diane is walking funny, we know what that means." He then turned around, looked at me with a big gigantic smile on his face, and turned back to her as they were walking on their way. I took that as confirmation that yes, he did the nasty with her and he liked it! I know this is all strange and out of line that a nine-year-old girl is thinking, saying, and shouting all these inappropriate things to her older boy cousin, but I just wanted to be sure he will then get what he wants from her and he could finally let me be. His new girlfriend had no idea that she had saved a nine-year-old girl from the trauma of incest molestation acts on her by her boy cousin.

Now that time has passed, the girlfriend is no longer with my cousin anymore. I don't know what happened to their relationship, but we stopped seeing her coming around like we used to. The reason why I knew that they probably broke up is because one night, when I was asleep in my grandmother's room, I was lying on the floor on a palate I created and I heard his footsteps coming toward the room, but for some reason, this night he turned back around because I think someone had called him to do something for them. I was never in a deep sleep when I did go to sleep, and this night, I ended up going to sleep a little bit late so I probably just dozed off to still hear footsteps, and as I looked up, I saw it was him walking off. It was the summertime, so the next morning, I went on my regular day, did all my chores, played outside with my friends, ran to the store if there was any, and took a bath and went to sleep. Then I thought to myself, I haven't seen my cousin all day, but what if he comes back, so let me wrap myself up in my sheet (head and all to prevent any spider bites or creepy crawlers from crawling on my face while I'm asleep) and sleep under my grandmother's bed. In this way, when he comes in, he might think that I spent the night at my friend's house or something.

I finally felt the all-clear to now get me some sleep to rest up for the next day (I loved the summertime and playing with my friends). In the middle of some good rest, I thought I was dreaming but still tried to force my eyes open to make sure what was happening was real. I felt my body sliding across the floor from under my grandmother's bed to the open floor. That's when I woke all the way up and pulled the sheet from over my head to look up and see my cousin pulling the tail of the remaining sheet at my feet. The way he was pulling me across the floors was as if he was hauling a wagon to a particular destination. I started crying saying, "No, cousin! I don't want to go! Stop!" But he continued to drag me from my grandmother's room, through the hallway to the bathroom.

Now that I couldn't talk him out of it, I found myself on the bathroom floor once again with the light on as bright as day. He was telling me to be quiet because I was crying with my hands over my face and he didn't want me to wake anybody up. So as he was pulling my pants down, I let my hands down from over my face to see what was in store for me, and to my surprise, I saw on the side of me cooking oil in the container it came in. I was confused, scared, and uncomfortable. The bathroom floor that night was not clean, and it felt like everyone in the world could see us, but they didn't say a word or make a sound. The world became still.

As he was licking me on my coochie, all I could do is stop crying, try to relax, and block everything that was happening in my mind with high hopes that whatever he wanted and was going to do to me would just be over with. The more relaxed I became, the longer he seemed to take! I became frustrated again and started crying and kicking, trying to get him off me. He must have realized that he needed to hurry up because I was making a scene. Somehow he managed to rub the cooking oil on himself, and with one hand holding both of my hands together over my head and used his body size and length to rub his private over my privates. He continued to do that until he released his slimy stuff on me! Finally, when he was done, he let me go. As I was crying, walking back to my grandmother's room, he nervously asked me if I was okay. I responded with, "Yes, I am okay," because I felt sort of bad for him the way he looked at me as

I was walking away as if he finally realized he had done something wrong. Maybe he thought I was going to tell someone because he noticed how sad, frustrated, and fed up I was. Telling on my cousin was not an option because I felt that if I were to tell, I would get separated from my siblings whom I dearly loved, and I didn't want anybody to be mad at me for snitching on him.

I knew my cousin was a drug dealer, so I felt that in due time, he'd get arrested for drug charges, and then I would finally get my break.

Can We Just Be?

In this time in my life, there was a very big change for our immediate family. I am now a ten-year-old girl who seemed to have her family back intact once again thanks to our guardian angels. I call them that because they owned some rental properties around Oakland and decided to give my mother a chance to live peacefully and normal with her five children by moving us into our own place. They offered their help to my mother because they knew that she really loved her kids but just needed a support shoulder and a fresh start to get her back on the right track again. Life had been tough for my mom and a serious struggle nonstop her whole life as she was the oldest of thirteen siblings with whom she helped raise them. As a grown-up woman, she graduated college, got married to my father who abused her, bore four girls with him, he introduced her to drugs, which then she struggled with drugs, finally broke free from him, met someone new, had a son with him, didn't work out because of his drug use and abusive ways, moved back with her mother for a place to stay with her children, that was no better for her because she lived alongside four of her siblings who used the same drug, which had to make it hard for her to stay clean.

So once again, a different support system was set in place for my mom and her children by ways of our other great uncle and great auntie who had a heart to help us out. As usual, this transition came with rules as to how my mother and us children should behave to maintain the help that they were giving us. My mother was to stay clean, have us in school, we were to regularly do Bible studies to stay in the word, and keep the property nice, clean, and pay the rent.

That was pretty darn reasonable for us as we were excited about the move, the location, and the place. We were now new residents on Seventy-Sixth Hamilton Street in Oakland. After a few months of my mother being clean, they also gave my mom a car for us to get around in. It was an old school car, almost a classic car that we used to make fun of and call it the SanFord and son olden day car! We were grateful for having a vehicle to get around in, so don't get me wrong, but the car was so old school that we hid down deep in our seats when our mom dropped us off at school. Even when we were driving around the neighborhood for grocery shopping, etc., we still hid whenever we thought we saw our friends or school peers. We used to laugh so hard that we even made a game out of it. When my mom noticed what we were doing, she laughed so hard with us that she'd purposely drive down blocks where she knew we had friends living, to embarrass and as a joke on us. She laughed so hard that we laughed so hard with her. We had so much fun doing that; it was the mom that she truly was, and even though that car had broken down, I felt that my mother had finally found peace and joy within herself.

The move into that house was such a wonderful time for us because we finally were able to have groceries that we didn't have to share and hide material possessions, have our mom full-time, no loud arguing of the grown-ups, we could have our things the way we wanted in our room, we had shared beds, but we had beds, and last but not least, no more hiding, dealing with the torture of sexual abuse from my cousin, and the fears of him finding my new hiding spots at night. No more rude awakenings. I felt like I was in heaven and can be free at last.

Everything seemed so perfect at this point in my life as a child. I attended Lockwood Elementary where I did all types of activities besides going to class every day, such as being a conflict manager, a captain of traffic class, and I was a captain of the school's drill team. I was living it up, having a normal childhood with high hopes of getting good report cards to show my mom.

Every morning that I went to school, a black cat with big yellow shiny eyes used to follow me from our house. It was a big shiny black cat who used to come up to me, rub its head against my legs while purring; as I continued walking, it followed me along to school. The most beautiful black cat that I've ever seen! My mom and all my sisters were cat fanatics; we all had a love for cats but never had one of our own. So one day, when I got home from school, I told my mom about this big cat. I described the cat to her by telling her that the cat favored a panther and that the cat was so nice that I think it likes me. She told me that the reason why that cat follows me to school is because she feeds it tuna in the mornings while we are getting dressed. I was so happy to know that she liked the cat because that gave me hope that she already had thought about having a pet. So in an excited voice, I asked her, "Momma, so can we have the cat as our pet? Can we have it in the house with us?"

She replied with a smile on her face, "Yes, we can have the cat, it's already been our cat! The only thing about it is that if we keep kitty in the house with us, we'd have to hide it when Aunt Myra and Uncle Roosevelt come over to visit us."

So we all were excited and thanked our mommy so much about letting us have a pet! I was curious as to what gender our new cat was after holding it and wiping it off with a towel. I asked my mom what kinda cat it was, girl or boy? She told me to lift the tail, so I lifted the kitty's tail. She then told me to check to see if kitty had anything hanging from the butt part. I said, "No, Momma, I don't see nothing but that yucky pink little round thing."

She laughed at me and said, "It's a girl then!"

I was so happy to know that, so after the good laughs, my momma asked me if I gave it a name already, and I said no. She said, "Well, what do you want to call it?"

I said, "Well, her face looks like a mama's face, and you told me that she likes tuna, so I'll call her Mama Tunie!"

My momma laughed and said, "Alicia, you are so smart. I like that name, so that's her name!" My mother made me a happy little girl that day. I was so happy it was all like a dream come true! My prayers have been answered.

We were finally a normal family, and my mother used to make the best dinners every day of the week. Our favorite that she used to make us for dinner was her shake and bake BBQ chicken with rice, corn, and her tasty sweet jiffy cornbread. Umm, mmm, mmm, it was so good!

I was loving my life as a child. I was getting good grades, having a good time, enjoying the activities at school, and making new friends. My first friend at Lockwood Elementary was a Cambodian girl named Sauve. The reason why I chose to have a friend from a different culture is that I was afraid of having black friends because as a school conflict manager, my job was to help stop dramas or beef with kids who fought each other or didn't like each other. It was never other races at the school who fought each other but my own kind. I was not a punk or nothing like that, but I did hear through the grapevine that the sixty-nine village kids who attended the school didn't get along with other kids who weren't from their neck of the woods, and since I was fairly a new kid for Ninety-Sixth in Plymouth, I was skeptical about hanging around my own kind there.

I was told how they like to fight a lot and jump kids, and I believed it because what I had to help solve most of the time also was a big eye opener too. I wanted to be on my best behavior, and since I was a part of the school's role model functions, I didn't want to risk being kicked out of the programs that I was a part of. So I took my chances with Sauve. How we met was really nice.

One day in class, during our free time, I noticed Sauve sitting at her desk while everyone else was either talking to each other, going on bathroom breaks, and the like. Sauve and I were the only ones still in our seats. I was curious as to what she was doing because I noticed her many different color pencils and stack of drawing papers. I was just sitting, looking dumbfounded around the classroom because I had no friends and I wanted to talk to somebody in class instead of sitting there looking stupid. So I was bold enough to get up and go to Sauve's desk and chat with her. As I was getting closer to her, I saw what looked like a pretty drawn girl's face on the paper in front of her. I was curious if she was the one responsible for drawing that art that captured my eyes.

Once she noticed me staring at her picture as I was approaching her, she said to me in the sweetest voice, "I drew this, do you like it?"

Happy that she spoke English, I replied back, "Yes, I do like it! It's a picture of a pretty girl, and it looks so real! I can't believe you drew that!"

She laughed and said to me, "Yes, girl, you betta believe it, I did that!"

I laughed back and asked her if it was okay if I sat with her, and she agreed. We asked each other's names, and she gave some paper and colored pencils and showed me how to draw the pretty girls. So we drew girls together until it was time for us to go back to our seats, and we became good friends. I teach my kids till this day how to draw those same pretty girls. Sauve introduced me to her cousins and other friends at lunchtime.

They did not speak English, and they kinda gave me the side-eye that made me feel a little uncomfortable. I asked my friend if everything was okay, was it cool for me to hang out with them or what? She turned her back to her crew and said, "Yes, you are too cool to hang out with us, my cousin just not okay with it, but you are cool with me so just stay with me." I really didn't like that, but Sauve was so nice to me that I overlooked her cousin's discomfort toward me and just stayed and only spoke with Sauve while we were with her crew. She was so sweet to me the whole time we hung out; she even showed me how to do a Chinese jump rope! One day, she even brought some Cambodian snacks to try. It was kinda nasty, so we laughed together as we were eating the snacks because it took me some getting used to and my facial expressions said it all! We always drew together on the playground at lunchtime or was doing some type of artistic, creative stuff like making beaded jewelry and the like.

After a month or so went by, her relatives and friends had a meeting with her about me while I was standing there. I could tell it was about me because they made it obvious by pointing and rolling their eyes at me. Sauve really valued me as her friend because even though they were speaking their Cambodian language, I could tell that Sauve was defending me by shaking her hand and head at them as if she was saying to them, "No! No! No!" As she was getting frustrated at her crew, she took a deep breath, pulled me toward her, and said, "Come on, Alicia! You are my friend, let's go by them because they are trippin'!" I stopped as she was pulling me to her as we were walking away, and I said, "Sauve, don't worry about me, but I am not going to hang with you if they are mad at you for playing with me!" I went on to say to her, "This is not right! Your family doesn't like me hanging out with you. I don't like how your cousins keep rolling their eyes at me, and I think I am causing you trouble between you and your crew! Sauve, thank you so much for being my friend, but we should just let it go. I will be okay!"

After I said that to Sauve, she was very upset with me and told me to not let them punk me like that. She just didn't understand that I did not want to be where I wasn't wanted and how it bothered me. So I walked away from Sauve and told her to go back with her family, just forget about me, and that I'll be all right. She stomped away mad at me and did not speak to me the whole rest of the school year as if I never existed to her in class. I still think about her from time to time and wonder if I hurt her feelings. She was my first real friend that was of another nationality. So after Sauve, I tried to stay to myself and stay focused on my grades.

The Lookout Kid

One day at school, I was on the playground just watching all the other kids play with their crews, then a Mexican girl wearing lipstick walked to me and said, "What's your name?"

I replied back, "Alicia! What's your name?"

She replied back with a smile on her face and said, "Maria!"

I then told this young lady how she looked like the high school kids, that she didn't look like she belonged in elementary school. She was just a year older than me, but she looked every bit of a sixteen-year-old girl. She had on a lot of makeup, and her hair was hair-sprayed up like a grown woman! She was somewhat desperate to get me to hang out with her; she too didn't have any friends. I felt that it would do me no harm to become friends with her and hang out with her at lunchtime. She seemed as if she was in the same position as me because we both did not have any friends, and why not give it a whirl to be nice and make a friend.

So we became friends only during lunchtime. One time at school, halfway into the lunch break, Maria seemed really anxious to find me because she was running toward me with this guilty excited look on her face. When she was finally close to me, she said, "Alicia, where have you been? I've been looking all over for you?"

I replied back to her in question, "I've been sitting right here the whole time. Where have you been?"

In excitement, she said, "Come! Get up! Let me show you where I've been and who my boyfriend is!"

As she was tugging and pulling me along with her, I was trying to figure out who is and what is this girl talking about! As we were getting closer toward where her boyfriend was, I noticed that the area she was taking me to was restricted for the Lockwood students to hang out or be at.

This feeling started to come over me that I would get in trouble if we were busted by the yard teacher for going to that particular area. This I knew because I was a part of the school's traffic and safety functions committee. As I was running with her to that area, I was looking around, paranoid, hoping that no one saw us.

I said to Maria, "We cannot go over there, Maria. We are going to get in trouble!"

She replied back as we were both huffing and puffing from running, "No, we're not! I've been coming over here, and I always make sure no one is looking when I come over here, and that's why I run fast when I notice the yard teacher over by the monkey bars!" Then she went on to say, "I know what I'm doing! You won't get in trouble, watch!"

I didn't give what she had to say to me much thought because I liked her as a friend. She was always nice to me, and she just seemed so happy, so I, being a kid in my stupor, continued with her to meet her boyfriend.

The way that the elementary school playground was set up is that it was adjacent to a high school called Havenscourt High School playground as well. The high school was on a different street from Lockwood Elementary, but the playgrounds were connected together, just divided by a wire gate. The reason why this one particular area was restricted is because someone cut out a body-sized hole in the gate, which was risky for the students due to either high school kids entering through or the elementary kids exiting the premises. That area was an escape route for high schoolers who periodically skipped school to go through the Lockwood playground to the street.

Now that we were where we shouldn't be, her boyfriend ducked through the hole in the gate and went to her, speaking in Spanish to her, hugging her, and tongue kissing her down! I was just standing there like an idiot, scared out of my mind, thinking to myself, *Oh my God! What have I gotten myself into?*

"I hope we don't get caught! I'm going to be in so much trouble!"

Maria stopped kissing her boyfriend while she was still hugging and holding on to him, looked over to me, and said to him, "Poppy, that's my friend, Willa, she's going to look out for us while we get to see each other." Then she continued on to say to him, "She's cool, she has our back, she's my friend!" She then looked over at me and said, "Ain't that right, Willa? You're going to make sure we don't get caught by looking out for the yard teacher, okay?"

I, being a little follower, said back to my so-called friend in a disturbed and upset voice, "Yeah, Maria! Go ahead! I'll keep a look-out and let y'all know when the yard teacher comes close!"

I felt like such an idiot. I felt used and betrayed of what I thought was a beautiful friendship with her! I was standing there on the side of the stairs across from the restricted gate area as a lookout girl for them so they could fondle, kiss, and play with each other instead of doing what normal nine and ten-year-olds do during lunchtime! I wanted to cry! I was very sad because I couldn't get the courage to just walk away and never deal with her again. I really felt for her because I saw how happy she was.

On one occasion at school during lunchtime, Maria found me and seemed really excited. I asked her what she was so happy about. She didn't respond right away, but she started looking in her back-pack as if it was a true emergency to find what she was looking for.

I said, "Maria, what's going on? What are you looking for?"

Maria said in a nervous voice while still digging around in her backpack, "I can't find my lipstick and eyeliner, where is it? I know I brought it!"

I was thinking to myself in a sarcastic way while she was on her search mission, *This girl is probably about to see her boyfriend today... great!*

So now that she found her makeup, she said to me, "Willa! You look too much like a little girl, so let me put some eyeliner and some lipstick on you because my boyfriend wants to meet you!" She then went on to say, "Girl, he is cute!"

I started laughing and said, "Maria, I don't want to hook up with his friend, how old is he, like seventeen?" I went on to say, "I am only nine years old, Maria, he's too big for me!"

She responded, "Willa, he is only sixteen, he is not too old for you. My boyfriend is seventeen, and that is the kind of boyfriend you should want, Willa, my friend, an older cute one! Mine buys me lunch, and the little boys won't be able to do that!"

I laughed at her and asked Maria, "Is he really cute though like you said?"

She said, "Come on, let me hook up your face, and let's wait until the yard teacher heads toward the back and run over there, they should be waiting on us."

I couldn't believe I let her talk me into doing that! I felt like since she did like my presence around unlike the other kids so far at school, so I wanted to try and impress her by looking and being mature like her. I also had a silly rebellious feeling that since I was going with her over there anyway, why not join the shenanigans instead of being the paranoid lookout girl. I'd feel better about it! I was so confused and nervous!

We finally arrived at the boyfriend meeting spot, and lo and behold, there was a cute Mexican boy standing there with Maria's boyfriend smiling at me!

I asked Maria, "Is that him? He is very cute!" This was my first time into boys, and I felt like a big girl for that moment. I didn't even care about the yard teacher busting us anymore, and I also felt a sense of puppy love at first sight! I looked over at Maria, and as usual, he ducked through the gate, went over to her, gave her some lunch, she and her boyfriend were kissing and fondling around. I looked over at the boy, and in disgust, I said, "I hope you don't think I'm kissing you like that? You're cute and all, but I don't get down like that!"

He laughed and responded with a question, "What's your name?" He then introduced himself and said, "You're cute and funny, my name is Louis. Maria told me all about you." He questioned me again and asked, "So you don't like older boys or something?"

I was very shy to him when he spoke because not only was he cute, but he seemed like a gentleman, very nice and not like his friend. I replied to him, "No! It's not that! I just don't really want no boyfriend right now. I'm only in the fifth grade!"

He chuckled and said, "You are in fifth grade? Wow! You don't look like it. Why won't you tell me your name?"

When Louis stated that I looked older, I hadn't had time to see what Maria did to my face, so I assumed she made me look like a little lady with the makeup on. I replied and said, "My name is Willa. Why don't you have a girlfriend already?"

He was reluctant to tell me, which made me assume he had a girlfriend already. As I started to walk away from them, he asked me, "Where are you going? Are you leaving?" and "Can I get a hug?" I was so shocked that he wanted to hug me because he was so much taller than me. I was scared to hug him, but I worked up the courage to go over to him and hug him.

Louis said, "Thank you, Willa! See you tomorrow?"

He said my name in Spanish, which I thought was cute, and I thought I was all grown and replied, "Maybe?"

As he started to reply, I heard the five-minute bell ring, and I got nervous and yelled at Maria, "We have to go now, Maria, the yard teacher will come this way to go toward the lines, let's go!"

She was nervous too and kissed and hugged her boyfriend good-bye, then we started running and peeking our way back to the proper areas of the playground.

I almost forgot that Maria put makeup on my face, and she looked at me and said, "We have to go to the bathroom, girl, and wash your face!"

I was happy she reminded me about that because if I would've gone home with makeup on my face, questions were bound to arise. I didn't want that, so we ran to the bathroom and cleaned my face with liquid soap and water to leave no evidence of makeup behind. As we were cleaning my face off, a feeling came over me, and I thought about my mother and said to Maria, "I don't want to go over there with you no more. Can we still be friends? Because I really like you, and you're the only friend that I have."

She replied, "Yeah, we will always be friends, but why are you not going back with me? Did Louis say something bad to you or something?"

I then explained to Maria that he was very cute and nice, but I can't help but to think about my mom if we got caught and what we were doing that it would hurt her, so I wanted to stay far from that gate, those boys, and not take any more chances.

She was mad at me and said, "We will always be friends, Willa, but I can't hang with you because I love my boyfriend, and this is the only way I get to see him at school, so I'll just see you when I see you. Okay?" Then she went on to say, "You don't have to see Louis, you can do like you've been doing and keep watching out for us. Would that make you feel better so we don't get caught?"

As the bell was ringing for all the students to line up, I didn't have time to really respond to her, so I told her that I would see her that following day, and we'll talk then. I only saw Maria at lunch-time. That was our only time together. So as I was running to the line, she was yelling, "We'll talk then, Willa, and don't forget about what I said!"

I yelled back, "Okay!"

The very next school day, I actually was looking for Maria this time, and I found her walking toward the bathrooms. I called, "Maria!" as I chased after her. I finally caught up with her and asked her if she wanted to talk, and she agreed to talk after using the bathroom.

So when it came time for us to talk, she asked me, "So are you coming with me or what?"

I said, "No, I can't remember what I told you yesterday. I feel bad for what I'm doing!"

She had an attitude and replied back, "Welp! Don't talk to me no more and move outta my way, Willa! You ain't my friend no more! Bye!"

I was so shocked because she said the day before that we'd always be friends. I felt so stupid because I really thought she liked me. She was basically using me the whole time as I initially thought.

The way she said it sounded as if she were saying, "If I can't use you to help me out, then get out of my face, you're not even worth me talking too!" That hurt my feelings that I actually cried because I thought it didn't matter about me being a watch-out person. I thought she started to like me as a person. Once again, a broken friendship, but that one was for my own good even though I was just a child, so I didn't see it that way. Sure enough, I held my head high with my feelings in the mud, kept it moving, and was by myself, alone all over again. I didn't want any friends, and I liked it that way.

Now that time had passed, my grades were good, traffic school was rewarding, I removed myself from being a conflict manager, but I was still captain on the drill team. My mother was doing good. Our house stayed nice and clean. My cat had kittens, and all was well.

This particular day at school, I was walking with my head down, and I accidentally bumped into this girl. I looked to her and told her that I was sorry for bumping into her. She rolled her eyes and said with an attitude, "*Excuse you, blackie!*"

I hated being called blackie, so I replied to her and said, "What do you call me?"

She, without hesitation, said, "I said excuse yourself, you tar baby!"

Now that she said that, all the other kids started gathering around and laughing at what she called me, watching us, and all I heard from the crowd was oohs and ohs! I felt that if I didn't say anything back, I'd look like a punk and then I would have to worry about getting bullied from other kids if I didn't stand my ground.

So I had to think of something quick, and I said back to her, "Yeah, I may be black, but at least I'm not a bald-headed bitch like you!"

Then all the kids started laughing and pointing at her, going and awing in an instigating voice, yelling, "Fight! Fight! Fight!"

So then she charged at me like a bull, and we both fell to the ground with her being on top of me! I then realized that I was now in a fight; now was the time to start hitting! All that I could do was keep hitting her in her head, hoping I'd hurt her so she could get off me. She didn't budge, so I kept hitting her head harder and harder, then a teacher pulled us apart. And she was so mad that she kept trying to break loose from the teacher to charge at me again.

The teacher yelled at us, "Both of y'all calm down! *Calm down!* We're going to the office right now!"

That day was a nightmare at school for me. I felt afraid to go back to school the next day. So a few weeks passed, and I kept hearing about the fight that I had with that girl in detail from different class and school students who witnessed the fight, describing how she fell on me, pinned me down to the ground, and about how I kept hitting her hard on her head. While these rumors kept circulating, and the gawkers were unsure of who truly won that fight, it was suggested that the same girl and I go for round two. She handed me a note when she walked past me in the hallway that read, "Meet me on the playground at lunchtime to fight!"

I ain't gonna lie, I was so scared because I heard that this same girl has five sisters, and I didn't know if she was gonna have me set up and jumped! So what's a scared little girl to do? I hid in the bathroom the whole lunchtime without lunch until the bell rang to line up for class. I took my precious time, petrified and on pins and needles, praying that she wouldn't spot me going to the line. Then voila! She spotted me and charged at me like a bull again, and there I went, smack hard into the ground, scrubbing up my back! We fought like there was no tomorrow, and again, there I was, hitting her in her head as hard as I could, and she's wrestling, twisting, and turning on top of me on the ground. I couldn't do anything but punch her as hard as I could! She was a strong little girl with a lot of anger and rage in her. I thought she wanted to kill me! The crowd filled around us and a parent who was there broke us up. While we were both getting dragged away by the adults, she hollered at me, "I'm gone really beat yo a—— next time I see! You betta watch out!"

I was so mad and scared that I didn't want to walk home by myself after school. That very next day, I faked my stomach illness to my mother so I could stay home. I took a can of pears and grape juice, smashed the pears in smooshy pieces and poured water and a little bit of grape juice in a cup.

I then poured a mouthful of this concoction, ran to my mother's room that early morning, and signed for her in an alarming way to come with me to the restroom. When she came into the restroom, I then spit up the juice out of my mouth in the toilet and faked cried, "Momma, my stomach hurt!"

She was frantic and felt sad for me as she thought I had come down with something, had me clean myself, and walked me to my room and had me lie down to get rest.

She said, "You're not going to school today, you're staying home!" She then went on to give me some water to sip on.

I was so happy that she fell for my sick trick! I felt saved and relieved for that one day. I saved the pears in the can under my bed and continued the same formula and played sick again the very next day as well.

I had no choice but to return back to school the third day due to the fact that my mother would need a doctor's note stating that I was too sick to attend class. I didn't want my mother to find out I was lying about my illness, so I had to face reality.

I waited to get to school until I knew the bell would ring, hoping she didn't go to school that day. Even though I needed a longer break from her, I knew somehow I was going to have to face this girl because she seemed so anxious about fighting me again, it's like she had a thirst for me! Kids kept telling me that she was looking for me and to watch my back. I was so scared and frustrated that I couldn't take the fears of her no more! It felt like she had me in some type of bondage. I couldn't eat, sleep, or focus on my schoolwork that the thought of her was distracting my whole life! I didn't want to tell my big sister about her because I knew what she'd do to this girl, and I knew that she had big sisters too! So I gave in to her madness and gained myself a pair of big balls that day! I searched for her that lunchtime with my heart on my shoulder as my heart raced but couldn't find her. The bell rang, school's out, I made it through the day without being terrorized by the vicious girl.

Lo and behold! She was standing under the monkey bars play area where I usually go through a gate to walk to the street. I had to walk down to get home. There was a small crowd with her, and I got scared again because I thought I was going to get jumped!

I nervously walked to her and said, "I don't know why we keep fighting, but all I want to do is go home!"

She gave me a cute chuckle and said to me, "Look, I don't want to fight no more, but we have to do this last fight and somebody has to win this one. I know it's gonna be me! So let's go!"

I then swallowed my heart down in my chest, my heart was beating so hard, I threw my backpack down, and put up my dukes as she raised hers.

We swung at each other like it was a battle for money! I got the most punches in that she bled on her face a little, and before I could get another good punch in, the yard teacher broke us apart.

As he blocked us standing in between us with his hands outward to keep us apart, he yelled at us, "What is wrong with you two?"

As I was going to just snitch and tell him that she kept starting fights with me, I felt my heart pumped so hard out of my chest like it was going to explode! I felt like a fish out of the water, and something took the air right out of me! I couldn't breathe, and I dropped to the ground as the yard teacher was trying to console me and yell, "Are you asthmatic? Do you have asthma? Do you have an inhaler with you?"

He was so afraid for me and yelled for someone to call the paramedics! I started to come back to normal and calmed down that I begged him or nobody else to call 911 because I felt better. He noticed that I was feeling back to normal, so he then looked at me and said, "Girl, all of this fighting done gave you an anxiety attack, are you sure you really don't have asthma?"

To my surprise, the girl and her onlookers hugged me and asked me if I was okay, and she said that she was sorry and did I want her to walk with me home. The yard teacher insisted that we just get along and work it out or we were going to get suspended. So while we were walking home, she told me that I had won the fight and she thought I was cool for putting up with her shit. She said that she was sorry and asked me a question that I thought I'd never hear from her, "Can we be friends?"

At first I was skeptical and thought she was trying to play me, but after that walk home together and the long talk we had that day, I felt we could be friends. I learned so much about her during that walk home. I found out that she had a lot of sisters just like me and that she was the youngest. She told me about how her mom smoked so much crack that they never have food; they were always scared of going to foster care and that her and her sisters had to steal food from Big T grocery store to be able to eat because her mom used their food stamps by selling them for drugs, alcohol, and cigarettes.

She told me how her oldest sister had to get a job to take care of the house. She was twenty years old. I gave her a big hug after our talk because I felt sad for her, but I wasn't comfortable telling her my problems. I was ashamed to tell her. So according to her, my life was good and functional. We were properly introduced to each other while we walked and talked, and I learned that she actually had a name: it was Beatrice.

Stealing Food on Training Day

Now that I've found a new friend (who started off as my enemy), we really connected on so many levels that I was blind to the fact that I was being led into doing things I know I shouldn't be doing. I felt so good about going to school knowing that I didn't have to fight again, that going to school seemed comfortable and assuring. On this particular day, my new friend and I decided that we'd walk home from school together. Beatrice's house was three blocks from the school, which meant her house came first before mine. So Beatrice asked me if I wanted to meet her sisters, and I responded to her, "Yeah!"

When we arrived at her house, I noticed that the house they lived in was a big-sized house that didn't look so bad on the outside. Once we entered her home, I noticed that it was empty of furniture. There was a love seat in the living room area and a kitchen table in the kitchen without the chairs. I thought to myself, *Wow! They don't have any furniture in here! At least we have nice furniture at my house!* I met her two oldest sisters, and they were short in size, and they all looked so much alike! They were really nice and welcoming, not the way other kids at school described them or how I imagined they'd be! They were dressed really pretty, and their hair looked as if they got it done by a hair beautician.

I was impressed by their attire and how well-dressed they were that I told them that they were very pretty and that I liked their hair. Now Beatrice, on the other hand, was more of a tomboy and very rugged with her looks and grooming. She was dressed more like a little boy than a little girl. Her hair was short, and she looked as if she barely combed it most days. She didn't like beads and bows, she explained to me once before. Her hair barely brushed into a full ponytail, and she always wore large-sized T-shirts, sagging jeans, and tennis shoes. Beatrice was the total opposite of her sisters. She told me that day her sister got paid from work, and she gave her five dollars to go spend at the store. I was happy for her because I knew that she was happy that they could eat good that day.

She offered to give me two dollars of her money, but I declined it because I knew she needed that money more than me. I was so anxious to take the money, but something just held me back from wanting to take it. In our time of friendship, I never got the chance to meet her mother because she was never there when I walked her home. I left her house to go home because I didn't want to worry my mom. As I walked the rest of the way toward my house, I was singing the whole two blocks home because I was happy that I had someone to walk me home halfway there and that she really was going to share with me some of her money. No friends that I've had ever offered me money before that I was so excited about that, especially because I know she needed it more.

After a couple of weeks have gone by, one day after school, Beatrice seemed confused about walking straight home from school. We always walked a straight path to take home and never switched up our walk home routine. This particular day, we walked past the neighborhood grocery Big T, and she had us stop. She gave me a puzzled look and said, "Willa! Let's go to the store!" The way she said it was as if she wasn't really sure about going to make this store run. So of course, by her being my friend and she'd usually have extra money to share for the both of us to spend, I U-turned around to go to the store with her, excited and without any doubt about it. I was actually planning to buy my little sister and little brother a sucker if Beatrice gave me some money to spend.

Once we got close to the store, Beatrice looked at me and said, "Alicia! We are friends, right?"

I said, "You know that! Why?"

She gave me this sorrowful look and sadly said, "You know I would not do anything to get you in trouble, but I am really hungry and my sister isn't working no more. Our mom took the food stamps we get and sold them to the D-boys up the street for dope, so we've been at the house hella hungry!"

My heart dropped to the pit of my stomach because I almost knew where this conversation was going. I felt so bad for her and her sisters that even though my mom and our household was facing hard times too, I did understand where she was coming from. I felt that we were in the same boat together.

So I asked her, "What are you thinking of doing?"

Beatrice seemed a lot more relaxed and competent after I asked her that question and then she went on to ask me if I've ever stolen anything from a store before, asking me the question to see if I was going to need her pointers on how to steal without getting caught.

So I told her, "Yeah, I did when I was five years old, I used to steal candy bars from Safeway until my mom and I got caught."

She laughed and said, "You don't seem like the type that would steal, you seem too scared to do something like that!" She then went on to say, "Y'all got caught? Dang! That's messed up! I can show you how I do it without getting caught, I steal from Big T's all the time and never get caught. I stole those cookies we had at lunch this morning before I came to school!"

I was confused because she had lied to me during lunch while we were sharing the cookies she just told me she stole. She told me that her sister brought her the cookies and thought she'd bring them to school to share with me because I was her best friend; that was her initial story. Had she told me she stole them, I would not have walked with her home because I was smart enough to know she'd want to steal again after school. I felt somewhat betrayed, but at the same time, I understood why she didn't tell me the truth at first because maybe she felt it would have ruined our friendship, and she probably was really embarrassed to tell me her truths. I took all that into account and proceeded to get instructions from her on how we were about to rob this grocery store. So now at age ten, and Beatrice was eleven years old, we were outside of a store, plotting its demise.

We were in the store pretending to be shopping for our parents, but we were really staking out the place to see if there were any store security guards and head persons paying any attention to us. Once we noticed that the store was good and clear of any deterrents, we took turns taking what we felt we needed for our family. When I saw how she stole, it didn't look that much different from how I had stolen before, but the difference was she was stealing meat packs and boxes of Rice-A-Roni! I was only used to stealing candy bars, two at the most three at a time. I was so shocked because she was stealing way too many packs of meat and all I kept thinking was, *Oh my gosh, if we get caught, we're actually going to jail!* She was stuffing steak, pork, and chicken packs in her pants; it had to be at least seven packs! I looked at her with fear in my eyes and talked to her with my eyes, saying, "Hurry up! Please finish what you're doing!"

She walked past me fast looking really full and fat then said quickly in a whisper, "I'm almost done, I just need some rice! You go next!"

I was so scared that I almost wanted to cry. I didn't want her to notice me whimpering up, so I kept a straight face while my heart was pounding through my rib bones! I thought I was going to have a heart attack, and I just died (that was what I was hoping would happen just to get out of it)! So many questions were going through my mind, things out of nowhere, wondering as to why was she my friend, was this why she always wore big clothes, we're going to get busted, we're going to juvenile hall, was she using me all along, why me God; these were all the things running through my mind before I got tagged to go do my turn while she looked out for me to steal. We had this code sound we were to make if someone were to come to the aisle we were stealing in. The warning code sound that we were to make was "Achoo!" a really loud fake sneeze sound. If we were to hear that sound, we would hurry up, tuck the item, and to just act regularly.

At this point, I was really rethinking the whole plan and was afraid out of my mind to take anything, so I didn't take anything. I didn't tell her that I didn't steal anything; I just played like I got what I wanted so we could leave. I wanted out of that place! It felt like a cold scary hell with food on the walls! I've never felt like that before, and I wanted to just go and hide myself under a rock somewhere. All

I could think about was my mom and how well she was doing at this time and that this would be the last thing that she needed. If I were to be caught and in trouble, would that cause my mom to relapse? That was a big question that kept popping in my head while flaking out of the plot.

Once we were out of the store, I almost fell apart and hugged her as if we just escaped a kidnapping and made it out alive! She was telling me while we were walking to her house how much she appreciated me being there for her and watching out so she could get her and her sisters some food for a couple of days. She told me that she wouldn't have been able to do it by herself. She then went on to ask me if I was cool and got everything I wanted. I gave her this look of frustration, and in fear, I told her, "You know I got your back, B, but I was too scared to take some food because I saw how much meat you got, and I didn't want us to get caught because you were taking too long!" I then went on to say and ask, "I never seen anyone steal that much stuff before. You're not scared?"

She answered me with laughter in her voice and said, "Girl, you don't think I'm a pro at this? I've been doing this for a minute, and I don't get caught! What do you mean?"

I was confused when she said that she's been doing this for a while, but at first thought, before we went into that store, I was under the impression that she was new at doing this.

I gave her this sad look and told her, "I am so glad that we are friends, but I can't be doing this stealing thing. I'm scared we will get caught and my mom will get in trouble by my aunties. If they find out that I've been stealing, they will kick us out of the house!" Of course, that wasn't going to happen to us, but I figured if I said that to her, she'd care enough to not ask me to steal with her again.

She felt some type of way about putting me in that position, so she gave me two packs of meat as we were walking up to her doorsteps. I was so happy that we didn't get caught and also happy that I was able to bring some meat home that Mom can use for our dinner that day. She always made the best baked meats.

When I got home, my mom was in her room watching TV with my two youngest siblings. My other siblings had not made it home from school yet, so I showed my mother the meats and told her that my friend gave them to me from her house. She was grateful for it and told me to thank my friend and her mother for the two packs of meat. I was happy because my mom was happy, and she got up to go into the kitchen to look for some other foods to put together for our dinner. My mother made the best cornbread, so I was happy that she said she was going to make beans, rice, and cornbread to go with the meat for dinner that day.

Dinner was always an important meal of the day and also a part of our family time together. Sometimes we ate at the table, and sometimes our mom lets us eat on the front room floor to watch comedy family shows while we ate. Television shows at that time had so many good morals and messages in them. As the saying goes, "Those were the good ole days!" I enjoyed laughing while watching those shows with my mom and siblings when we did watch TV. The comfort of feeling like an intact family was always a great feeling to me. I felt normal, comforted, and loved when we were together with each other, it felt so peaceful. My mom always seemed to find a way to make sure that we ate good dinners.

When we ran out of food stamps, my mom wouldn't hesitate to find out what churches or neighborhood programs were giving away free food. We'd walk to that place no matter how far, rain or sun, with our own plastic bags, with high hopes of coming up with a bunch of free groceries from somewhere. No matter how she had to do it, she made sure we always had those dinners. In those good family times, she'd always prepare us a three-course meal, the meat, a carb side dish, veggies, and if we were lucky, cornbread or homemade biscuits with juice. Just so good! My mom was doing so good, and our family didn't need no interruptions at this point in time even if it meant that I had to cut my only friend off who was going to eventually get me into unwanted trouble.

So the next day, when I went to school after our robbery session, she didn't show up to school. I was somewhat relieved because I was about to cut off our friendship. I was always open to having friends at school but afraid to have friends at the same time. The neighborhood I grew up in was very rough, and everybody was struggling in their own way; I knew that dealing with anyone outside of my siblings would be risky because I just never knew who was who and every friend that I met at Lockwood was always up to no good. Everyone had their own problems in their own ways, and watching your back was a thing of that time and place.

Dealing with friends always seemed to have landed me in some type of trouble one way or the other. I was hoping to end my relationship with B and focus on schoolwork. I saw B that following day, and she was acting very strange. We hugged and greeted each other like we normally do, but this day, she looked as if she didn't get any rest.

I asked if she was okay, and she said, "Yeah, I'm okay!" but I didn't believe her, and I just let it go. I was debating on telling her how I felt about our friendship and that I didn't want to hang out with her no more, but I didn't think it was the right time to tell her that, so we continued on with our school day. Once the bell rang for us to get out of class, she was anxious and excited! I had a gut feeling that this girl was about to ask me to go steal again from Big T's!

She kept talking about her sisters and her mom, how they were happy about the food she brought home the other day. I felt like she was trying to play on my kindness because she knew how I felt about her siblings and situation. I had to cut her conversation toward me short, and I explained to her my life situation with my family. I never told her about my personal stuff because I was ashamed to tell her, but I had to share with her that information as a form of breaking off the relationship.

I told her, "B! Look! I know you have this thing that you do to help your family, but I can't be stealing! I already have my struggles and stealing is just going to make things worse, especially if I get caught! I can't walk with you home no more and maybe we shouldn't be friends either!"

She was so mad at me and also afraid that I would snitch on her if she let me know that she was mad at me for what I said. I noticed her confused look, so I tried to ease her mind by letting her know that I wasn't upset with her and I just wanted to do my own thing and keep to myself. She tried to still talk me into stealing with her at the store and said to me, "All you have to do is just keep an eye out on the store manager and if you see him coming, just do the sneeze thing really loud. I'll hook you and your family up!"

I asked her in return, "If you get caught, will you say I don't know you? So that way I won't get in trouble?"

She said, "If you keep your eye out on dude, and let me know he is coming my way, then you won't have to worry about that because we won't get caught!"

I was on pins and needles about the whole plot. I knew I should just follow my first mind, listen to my gut feeling versus thinking about the dinner that my family could have for that night and go on with her plan.

She kept trying to assure me that we weren't going to get caught and that this would be the last time she'd ask me to do her this favor. I was so on edge! I wanted to go with her to the store so bad, it was so tempting, especially since I knew she'd be the one pocketing and stuffing the food, and all I had to do was just look out. My flesh was willing, but I had a bad feeling about it. All I kept thinking about at that point was how much it would be my luck if I went through with it and we ended up getting caught on my last run with her.

After careful and paranoid thoughts, I opted out of her plot and told her that I still would say hi to her when I see her at school and that I would never tell her that that's her business, then I left even though she kept trying to persuade me to do it one last time. I left her talking to herself because I woke up and realized that this girl whom I thought was my friend was just a thief and had a lot of behavioral issues that were starting to have an effect on me. There was a good feeling that came over me as I walked away from her, the feeling of security that I knew she wouldn't want any beefs with me due to the fact that we already fought before and she knew that I wasn't scared of her.

I did feel so sad for her because I did take a liking to her, and I understood her situation; it was almost familiar to me, but I just couldn't risk thinking about being the person to mess up our happy home with my shady ways kicking with her. After cutting ties with B, it was sort of awkward seeing her in class without talking to her and not walking with her to go home from school. It took me a few weeks to realize that I did the right thing because unfortunately for my ex-friend, she ended up getting caught boosting clothes at a flea market on E14th Street and went to juvenile hall for it. I was aware of her situation because I overheard another classmate mentioning it to another classmate outside on the yard. I played the role as if I didn't hear what they said because I didn't want anything to do with their gossip. It had to be true because I hadn't seen her again after hearing that news. I did feel bad for what happened, but she already made up her mind that that was the lifestyle she wanted.

The New Member of the Family

Times have passed, and so far my mom was doing great and so was her children. I am still nine years old at this point of my life, and things took a hundred-and-eighty-degree turn. Living in the neighborhood that we were in had to be tough for my mom because she was surrounded by drugs as she was recovering and fighting temptation. We still had our black cat, got a new kitten, we met a new friend that lived in the same triplex as us. My mom became friends with her mom and her mother's siblings and our aunt moved to the triplex directly behind our house. Our house was actually the biggest house in our triplex area. The triplex consisted of three small houses that my great aunt and uncle owned.

What's Going On?

Our house was the biggest house on the lot, my younger aunt moved into the smaller house in back of us, and our newfound friends who had been living there longer than the residents of that area stayed in the medium-sized home that was located on the front street block of Seventy-Sixth in Hamilton. There was a gate that surrounded our premises that was always locked to keep intruders from entering. We used to have so much fun playing in the big yard, and every time some of the neighbors in our triplex needed some sugar, flour, tissue, etc. to borrow, everyone always loaned these types of items if they had it and was repaid back with either money, the same thing, or something different that they may have needed at the time. Everyone in the triplex was like one big happy family who looked out for each other.

It was fun living in the triplex area because our auntie lived right behind us; it was her, her baby's father, and their toddler. It was cool because we used to love seeing my baby cousin come over to play with us; either she'd greet us in the morning before we go to school or after we got home from school. For a while, my mother was doing great and staying drug-free, but that would soon change. While we were living in those triplex homes surrounded by relatives and good neighbors, I was so distracted from paying close attention to my mom for a while because at this point I now have friends to play with outside in the yard, and I felt that my mom was safe in our vicinity around loved ones and close friends. So I really never paid her any mind or felt the need to keep an eye on her to make sure that she was good. She had other people around for that. My mom, at some point, did slip up and was getting high again but doing it very discreetly. I didn't say anything to my mom about it even though I could kind of sense that she was because I noticed a few different people started coming to our house, including the neighbors, regularly and her room door was closed when they came over. She usually always kept her room door open, which was a good thing that she kept her door closed with company so in that way, whatever she was doing behind closed doors, we didn't have to know about it. It was okay as long as it was out of sight and out of mind, and she took care of the house. We'd just act like it wasn't happening because she would still function as a single house-mom, even though we knew she was getting high again. It really didn't bother me because I was just so happy that I didn't have to deal with my cousin anymore. I knew that my life would've been so much worse. I was content and humble.

This one day in particular, I was coming from the bathroom and decided that I'd go check on my mom to see what she was doing in her bedroom, especially since her friends weren't over and her bedroom door was closed. The hallway was a walkway in the house that connected most rooms in the house. The bathroom was in the middle of the hallway, so when you'd exit the bathroom, you'd either be walking toward the right to head to my mother's bedroom or to the left toward the kids' bedroom. Both bedroom doors were in plain eyesight once leaving out of the bathroom. There was also a wide doorway toward my mother's bedroom to the first left that connected to the living room area. Usually, she would introduce her company to us or make us aware that she has company over so that we wouldn't just barge into her room.

As I was walking closer to her room, I thought I heard a man in the room, but I couldn't tell if it was her TV or somebody actually in there with her; so I wanted to be sure just in case before I opened the door. I put my ear to her door and heard her say, "No, uh-uh! I really don't want to! I just can't!"

Then I heard a man's voice say, "Here, mane! Take it and stop playin'! It's all good!"

I was so curious about who this man was and why she didn't tell us about him, so I wanted to crash their party and introduce myself.

I was feeling a little rebellious, bold, and bad at that moment. So I went to push the door open and the small TV stand without the TV on it was in the way of me opening the door, so I kept pushing into the door until it cracked open. I saw this mystery man standing over my mother while she was sitting on the foot of her bed! He didn't see me because his back was turned toward my direction, and I don't think he heard me either because he didn't flinch. The room was slightly smoky, cloudy, and the room light was on even though it was daytime; when she noticed me looking through the crack, I quietly closed the door and ran hoping she didn't see me standing there! I didn't know what was going on in there, but I decided to just go on about my business and zip my lips and act as if I didn't see it. It was strange to me, and I couldn't help but to think and question the whole time after I saw them together. Why is he in the room with my mom and why was the door closed and what was all that smoke about? It was really strange, and I really didn't want to start anything that I would regret, so I let it go and tried my best to block it out of my mind. That was a hard thing to do, but after the weeks went by, I got over it.

As we played outside in the yard, there used to be this mentally ill older man; he was homeless and a wino who used to always stop and say things to our neighbor's parrot named Peewee. That parrot used to talk and sometimes repeat what the old drunk would say to him. The words were too rated R to say around us kids, but this old drunken man had a mental condition and we all knew that. We were ghetto kids who've seen and heard unthinkable acts, so when we saw or heard crazy people do crazy stuff, we usually just laughed at them. This homeless man who was a drunk in our neighborhood became a household name on that block. Everyone knew him as Uncle Buck the Drunk who usually went strolling the streets, bumming people for cigarettes and money. We became fond of him even though he always smelled really bad, reeked of alcohol, and said nasty crazy things because he always made us laugh and we knew that he was just out of his mind.

He always had this look of happiness when we called him over to our gate, and we could tell he liked that we laughed at his crazy ways, so he made it an every week thing to come to the gate to make us laugh. He was in a sense like our uncle that was crazy who none of the adults liked. Uncle Buck was about sixty years old, six foot in height, slim built, had only about two teeth in his mouth, brown skin in color, his right hand only had two fingers and had a permanent bend, he always wore a smashed low-cut afro, had a baseball cap that he loved to always wear cocked backward, and wore the same exact same clothes every day. We enjoyed seeing Uncle Buck when he came to the gate. At first, he'd come to the gate to see the parrot to mess with him, but he enjoyed making us laugh so he made it a thing to come over to say hi to us. Uncle Buck was something else. I don't know why, but I always had a heart for him. When he used to come to visit the bird, he'd say things to the bird like, "Pop that p——!" and made a popping sound with his mouth after saying that to the bird! Uncle Buck said that every time he spoke to the bird with high hopes that the bird would repeat what he said. I'm laughing now as I'm writing this remembering him. We kids always thought that what he did was so funny because we always laughed at each other and always asked each other, "Why is he saying that to Peewee? He does know that Peewee is a boy bird? Right!" We were confused but at the same time entertained. He said that every single time he came over to our gate to talk to the bird and he did this ritual every three days out of the week during the summer.

After a while, when Uncle Buck came by, we all greeted him with a loud and happy, "Hi, Uncle Buck!" He'd then go to say to Peewee the parrot (and we'd say it with him), "Pop that p——!" and we'd all do the popping sound at the same time! We'd all laugh so hard with Uncle Buck, and he'd just sip on his Thunderbird wine that was always wrapped in a brown paper bag. It became routine with Uncle Buck, but this one time in particular, the parrot wasn't outside for him to mess with. He looked over in the area where the bird normally hangs out and noticed that Peewee wasn't there. He then looked over at us kids playing then said out loud, "Pop that p——!" and did the popping sound. We didn't say it with him this time on that day nor did we laugh with him because our friend's mother was outside hanging out in the yard.

She heard what he had said to us, and she jumped up so quick and cussed Uncle Buck out so badly, calling him all kinds of perverts and pedophiles while throwing stuff at him. He walked away with his head slouched down, talking to himself, and started to drink on his Thunderbird. We felt so bad for him, and we had an obvious sad look on our faces. Our friend's mother looked at us and said, "How long has he been coming over here saying that to y'all?" with disbelief in her voice with a disturbed facial expression.

I said to her, "He comes over and says that all the time, but he doesn't mean anything by it though. He just likes Peewee!"

She looked at me like I was crazy, and I heard her say under her tongue, "Something is really wrong with this little girl!" So she grabbed her daughter from playing with us and walked away.

I was mad because we were outside having so much fun and I thought I told her the right thing to not be mad at Uncle Buck for what he did. I seemed a little off to her, and I didn't think she wanted her daughter to play with me no more after what I said to her in Uncle Buck's defense. So after that episode happened, she still allowed her daughter to play with me, Uncle Buck still continued coming to the gate saying his favorite saying to the bird, and we kept on laughing every time. One day, Uncle Buck came to the gate, and he didn't say anything. I thought maybe he was tripping and too drunk to say something. So I kept looking at him to see why he wasn't saying anything and just staring at us. I thought, *Uncle Buck is tripping!* and I was confused because the parrot was outside in his usual spot and he didn't try to go to him to say what he always would say to him. I got a little scared and concerned, so I went to the gate and I said to him (this was my first time saying something to him face-to-face), "Hi, Uncle Buck! You okay?" He stood there, standing really still, and dropped his head down fast! He then lifted his head up slowly, looked at me, broke out with this goofy silly dance, and started laughing so hard! We all started laughing so hard altogether that for that moment, he was like a really fun uncle that was just being crazy and silly! Unfortunately for us and Uncle Buck, he passed away two weeks later after that last visit.

When Uncle Buck passed away, we just hung outside and played with our neighbor who lived in the front triplex unit of us who was much younger than us. She had to be every bit of four years old while we were older ten- and eleven-year-old kids playing with her. Her mother was a crack addict and so was her aunt and uncle who all lived with their mother in a small two-bedroom place. I will never forget their mother who was a much older Caucasian woman who everyone in the neighborhood called Ms. Lokehart. She had three adult children Joni, Sonny, and Regina. The three adult children who lived with her had to be mixed because I could tell by the way the texture of their hair was that of mixed people's hair, so apparently, their father must have been a black man whom we've never met or seen before.

These neighbors of ours were actually really nice, and one thing that was different about one of those adult children who lived with their mother in the front of us was that she was a full-blown lesbian, which was my first encounter being around a lesbian, which in the hood we used to call lesbians dykes. She used to have a girlfriend called NaeNae, whom we met because Regina used to bring her to our house all the time. It was always fun seeing this couple together because I liked how different they were and they didn't have a care in the world of what anyone thought of them. They flaunted their relationship and love for each other around the hood as if they were boyfriend and girlfriend. Regina had to be the male of that relationship because she was really butchy and tomboyish, always wearing men's shirts and baggy jeans. NaeNae, on the other hand, had more girly ways and dressed really cute with Daisy Duke shorts and tank top shirts that had a tied knot at the bottom of them.

My mother became good friends with Joni, Sonny, Regina, and NaeNae. They'd frequent our home from time to time, and we were happy to see that our mother had some actual regular friends to entertain her. She didn't have a boyfriend or husband at this time, and it was just us kids who were her only company besides her smoker buddies. I never looked at those people as her real friends because they only used her to have somewhere quiet and safe where they could get high.

They were mostly working middle-class people who were undercover dope addicts. They were decent and very secretive, but my mother would get money and drugs from them so she would use them too. Seeing our mother interact with other people in our triplex made me feel like she could create her own family or circle. She didn't live close enough to her other siblings, just the one sister who stayed in the triplex unit directly behind our house. Anytime that Regina and NaeNae will come over to the house to visit our mom, she was always in a good mood. One time in particular, we were all playing outside with our friend who lived next door. We saw Regina and NaeNae go over to our house to visit our mother as usual, so I didn't think anything of it and continued playing outside until I got thirsty to run in the house to get something to drink.

When I went into the house and got my drink of water, I was standing in the kitchen with the cup of water in my hand, trying to decide which toys I should try to find out of my room to take outside to play with my friend. So once I was done with my cup of water and contemplating trying to kill some time, I finally thought of which toy or toys I wanted to go and find in my room. I went and opened my bedroom (which was adjacent to the kitchen) door, I then saw something that was different from what I've ever seen from two adult women. At first I thought it was unusual that our bedroom door was closed because, normally, we always kept our room door open.

There was the strange moment of silence and startled faces because once I opened the door, I looked straight ahead, and there I saw on my bed were two completely naked ladies on top of each other. I saw Regina on top of NaeNae with her head face coming from NaeNae's vagina and NaeNae's hands were holding Regina's head and looking right at me! When I saw that, I just stood there and stared in shock because I was a ten-year-old kid and I didn't know what I was looking at and I was scared to move! This was my first time ever seeing something like this! I didn't want to let them see me, but it was already out there in the open that I'm looking at them and they're looking at me stiff as statues in shock too that I was seeing them naked on top of each other and they see me looking directly at them!

So once I saw them looking at me and I finally jumped out of my numbness, I finally slammed the door closed and ran outside! When I got outside and saw my sisters playing with our friend, I didn't know how to tell them what I just saw because the neighbor who we were playing with which was our friend, it was her auntie and her aunt's girlfriend having sex with each other. We were having so much fun playing outside that I didn't want anything to ruin it because if I would have told my oldest sister that I just saw Regina and NaeNae having sex on my bed, she would have went off because they were in our room having sex! But luckily for my older sister, they were not doing it on her bed. It was on my bed that I shared with my other sister.

So at this point, I was so confused on what I should do, should I just wait to tell my sisters after we go inside and wash up for dinner, tell them about what I saw and joke about it, or just go all out and open with it and say what I saw even though the little girl that we were playing with was her auntie at hand who was using my bed. Everyone was having so much fun and I thought I'd just wait until me and my sisters go in the house and then tell them about it later, hoping we will have something to joke about privately among ourselves. Our friend was four years old, so I didn't want to make her feel sad about what her auntie was doing in our room. I also didn't know if she knew about her auntie being a lesbian and what that life was all about. My mother was probably in her room when all that was happening. I'm not sure because I didn't go check on her. I just ran directly outside after I saw what I saw.

So once we were inside and washed up, after we got through eating and we were in our room, I opened up to my sisters and them about what had happened. My oldest sister, as I suspected, went off and got up to go confront my mother about what I had said about what I saw in our room that day. I tried to calm my older sister down, but it was not working because she felt that she needed to say something to my mom because we were finally living a normal life and my oldest sister took that as a sign that maybe my mother was back using drugs again. Maybe my oldest sister felt that way because if she wasn't, why would our mom let these two ladies have sex in our bedroom while we're playing outside; she knew our mother would not just do that naturally. When my sister finally had a sit-down talk with my mother, my mother opened up to my older sister and told her that they paid her to use our room to have sex in.

My oldest sister was a little shook up by it all and was in disbelief about the situation, but at the same time, we were poor and my older sister felt that since she let them use our room, where is our cut since they used our room. My mother had to explain to my older sister that she was going to use that money to get groceries and wash our clothes at the laundromat the next day with it. So my sister was okay with the situation, and we all joked about it and laughed about it. Regina and NaeNae always sat in this chair in front of their place during the evening times of the day, and NaeNae was always sitting on Regina's lap. They were so in love with each other. After that incident, we would see Regina and NaeNae together sitting outside on a chair in their usual sitting position, and we would walk past them and stare at them as if we know what they really do.

Boyfriend

My mother was getting high but not as bad as she used to, and she was taking care of the house when she did get money, so she would go and find other ways to get money to support her drug habit by getting credit from the corner store D-boys. They were usually cool with my mom and would give her credit so that way she'd spend the money on the first of the month for basic necessities because government paydays were every first and fifteenth of the month. Monies spent on the first was for rent, wash, utilities, and bare necessities. Food stamps took care of the food. They understood that she had a bunch of kids to take care of, and they did want to keep her business because they knew she'd be good to pay them back on the fifteenth and also she'd pay back double of what she'd originally borrowed. She'd always promise to pay them back on the fifteenth. One day in particular, my mom couldn't get credit from her usual drug dealers because they weren't around the corner that day. So she decided to score from my oldest sister's boyfriend's homies for her dope needs. My oldest sister had a boyfriend who lived around the corner from us, and even though he didn't slang rocks, most of his friends did. They also knew the dope dealers that my mom used to score from.

When my sister's boyfriend came over to visit her, he used to come with his crew sometimes, which included a couple of his dope dealer male friends. How convenient for my mom because her regular D-guys weren't around on this day that she needed to score. Even though it was cutting it too close for my mom by purchasing dope from my sister's boyfriend's friends, unfortunately, she'd soon find out that switching drug dealers wasn't always a smart move. My mom had scored from one of his best friends named Daniel. She received credit from him and told him that she would pay him back on the fifteenth of the following month. A couple of weeks later, it was about the second of the next month, Daniel showed up to our home uninvited and banged on our screen door.

When my sister went to answer the door, she seemed shocked and asked, "Daniel! What are you doing here? Where's my boyfriend at?"

He didn't respond to her question, instead looked over her shoulder, looking through our door toward the living room and saying, "Where is your mom? Where's she at!" He was sweating and breathing hard as if he had been chased by somebody.

My sister said, "She is here! She's in the room sleeping! Why?"

He responded, "She owes me some money! Tell her to come to the door."

So we went to tell our mom what Daniel said, and as she was getting up to go to the door, she said to us, "I told him to come on the fifteenth to get his money. Why is he here today asking me for the money? He knows I don't have it! I already told him when to come!"

I explained to her that he looks really mad, so as she was going to the front door, Daniel bum-rushed his way through the door and came directly on in! As soon as he came in through the door and was close to my mom, he grabbed my mother by her throat and threw her down to the floor and started punching her in her face. We were screaming and yelling for him to get off of our mom, but he wouldn't get off of her! She was screaming and telling him, "I told you to come on the fifteenth that's when I would have your money," but he just kept on attacking our mom.

We ran to the kitchen to grab whatever we could grab! My sister grabbed the black skillet, and I grabbed a big pot, and we started hitting Daniel as hard as we could with the pots hoping we could get him off of our mother. Then it got too dangerous to the point where he put a chokehold on our mom, her face was turning red, and she could not breathe! So we screamed, pleaded, and begged Daniel to stop and please let go of our mom! My oldest sister dug her nails into

Daniel's skin while holding both of her hands around his neck. I kept on banging on him with the pot while crying and screaming, "Let go of our mom, please!"

So he finally let go and said while gasping for air, "Don't ever fuck with me again!" He then rushed out of the door, skipped over the four steps on the front porch, hopped over the gate, and ran!

We then closed the front door, locked it, held our mother, cried, and was holding her like she was a big baby. We felt so bad about what had happened that we were all in a state of shock. We were all so speechless for the moment. My sister assured my mother that would never happen again. My mother assured us, hugged us, and told us that we would never have to worry about that happening again, to just keep what happened between us, and to not tell anybody about what happened. My oldest sister couldn't keep what had happened between only us because she knew she'd see him with her boyfriend again and that he should be in the know about what his so-called friend did. So when she confronted her boyfriend about what one of his best friends had done, he told my sister and us that we didn't have to ever worry about him coming to our house and doing nothing like that again. He said that he and his other friends would take care of him and that they were going to beat him up for what he did because what he did was wrong and uncalled for. At first I thought that her boyfriend wasn't going to do anything about what Daniel had done because it was their friend who had done this terrible thing to our mom.

I just knew his response was probably going to be that our mom should pay him his money. Thankfully, in that part of the hood, Mommas who they knew, were off-limits from any acts of drug violence and especially because it's his girlfriend's mom, they really weren't feeling what he had done! My sister's boyfriend and his friends told us that Daniel would slip up and when they catch him, he will be dealt with. When he explained that to us, we felt safe and knew that we'd never have to worry about Daniel hurting our mom again. They also assured our mom that she didn't have to pay him anything back, that he just needed to charge that money she owed him to the game.

God Is Stomping on the Ground

Times had passed of that incident, and on this one particular day, something really strange, out of the blue that was so very scary had happened. This was by far the scariest day of my life at that time! I got home from school that day and everything was good at school. There were no unwanted distractions, no fights, no friends bothering me, I finally got to focus on my schoolwork, and all was well. I got home from school that day and was doing my homework. After I was done doing my homework, my mother let me come sit in the room with her to watch television. It was a usual routine for us to do our homework after we got home from school and then my mother would start cooking dinner on the stove, then we would go sit down on the floor at the foot of her bed to watch TV shows with her.

On this particular day, as we were sitting there and watching our favorite TV show just chilling and relaxing, out of nowhere, the floor started to jump up and down! So suddenly, the whole house started to shake up and down, all around, and my mother jumped out of her bed so fast, us kids were so scared; my mother told us to run into the hallway with her. Once we were in the hallway, she told us to stay still and hold on to the wall all while the whole house just kept on shaking and rocking! I was so scared that I was crying, and at the same time, I was praying that the shaking would stop.

It felt to me like God was mad at everybody on the planet, so he came down and started stomping his feet really hard, causing the ground to shake violently to wake us all up! As a kid, I felt that God was angry and this was his way of getting everybody to stop being bad and to be good. For some reason, even though the house was shaking all over the place, I wasn't worried not one bit that I was going to die. I knew that God wasn't finished with us yet. Once the shaking had finally stopped, you can hear people outside talking loud in shock, car alarms going off, cracking sounds of the walls in the house, and it seemed like the whole world was going to cave in! It was so scary, you can hear kids outside crying, and you can hear grown-ups outside screaming; it was total chaos! But during all the commotion, our mother stayed calm the whole time, not letting us see that she was scared to keep us comforted so that we would feel not-so scared.

She really hid it very well that she was scared, but deep in my heart, I knew she was and that she just wanted to stay strong and not be scared for us which really did work for me! She then escorted us outside to see if she got any information from anyone and to see if anything was damaged in our house. There were two tall houses that were directly in the front of our triplex facing the other street. The house at the corner was a three-story house which looked like an older Victorian home, and it was leaning to the side like it was going to fall! The other house that was in front of us only had minor damage that the earthquake had done to it which broke off several bricks from the rooftop chimney of that house. Inside of our house, we noticed about five long skinny cracks on our ceilings and walls, but that was the only damage that the earthquake did to our house.

Everybody patiently waited for the electricity to come back on because it was starting to get dark and my mother kept mentioning that she needed to see the channel 2 news. After that earthquake, a few aftershocks happened, and people were still staying outside of their homes. It seemed as if everybody was so scared to go inside of their homes because people were probably scared that their house was going to collapse on them! Once we had the third aftershock and a couple of hours had passed, my mother felt like it was safe to be inside and the electricity was finally restored. Once we got inside, I felt so uncomfortable being in that house that our home started to feel so scary to me. My mother had taken all the curtains down to get extra light in the house before all of the electricity was completely restored. I didn't want to go in the house. I almost started to hate being in the house and wished that we could have just had a tent to live in and just stayed outside where there were other people and nothing hard over the top of our heads. I was so traumatized by that big earthquake that scary day of October 17, 1989. I was really afraid because it happened in the evening, before it started to get dark outside. Once we were finally able to watch the news, we noticed that some people didn't make it out of that earthquake alive and that a lot of people died. Everybody in our neighborhood was safe; no one was injured or killed as a result of that big earthquake.

Unfortunately for other Bay Area residents and visitors from other places, they were injured, trapped in buildings, or killed due to collapsed buildings and or being caught on fire. Bay Bridge upper deck portion caved in, the Cypress overpass in West Oakland had completely collapsed, and the other saddest incident was the Embarcadero freeway which was the upper decker freeway level collapsed and killed a lot of people who were crushed in their cars. I was so sad watching the news with my mother because even though we were all safe in our neighborhood living our life back to normal again, houses were still habitable, and the electricity was working good again, there were still other people who lost their lives and relatives and friends were mourning over the death of loved ones or lost their homes and others still trapped in rubble. It was just a bad, terrible earthquake! I didn't get over that earthquake, and for a while, I still didn't trust the ground again after it because of what had happened. I just didn't know when it was going to happen again!

I actually hated watching the news because it kept showing sad stuff, seeing the blood on the bridges, freeways, blood leaking from cars. It was also scary and disturbing seeing the completely smashed cars and buildings that were on fire and the buildings broken all up in what looked like big broken bloody cement rocks. It was so depressing watching it on TV, so I really hated it when my mom would put on the news. I used to wish that she would just put on something funny that we could watch to get my mind off of what had happened. I never told her that because I was actually appreciative that she wasn't being afraid and getting the information that she needed. That earthquake was probably a wake-up call for her too!

Maybe she needed to see the damage that was done elsewhere to keep her humble and grateful that it could have been us.

It was kind of weird in our neighborhood because the house that was at the corner I mentioned was leaning, even though it was condemned by the city, the crackheads of that area kept finding ways to tear down the boards off the windows and doors of that house to get inside to occupy it. It was weird that they were living in that house that was leaning sideways because it looked like at any given moment, that house was going to tilt and fall over. It had big long two-by-four boards holding it up from the ground, and the city had yellow caution tape around the house and sidewalk so that nobody would walk on that part of the sidewalk or close by that house. You'd technically have to cross the street or walk in the street when going past that house just in case that house decided to fully fall. It was really creepy looking at that house, I was almost hoping that it would just hurry up and fall because it was a constant reminder of that earthquake on my walk to and from school.

Things were really different after that Loma Prieta earthquake while living at that house. My mother started using less drugs than before and was slowly but surely trying to quit. Now by this time, I started to become more mature, mind and body-wise. I was now growing breasts and getting my pubic hairs in various places on my body. I was ready to have a boyfriend because I figured that I was becoming a lady and wanted to do big girl things. My sister had a different boyfriend at this time, and I asked her to see if he knew any boys that were my age. She told me that he did have a little brother who was twelve years old. So next time her boyfriend came over, he was with his little brother, and his name was Lionel. We hooked up instantly when we met each other and became boyfriend and girlfriend. After several visits from my boyfriend, we started going to the side of the house where we were all alone to hold each other in a standing up cuddling way and kiss on the lips. We never tried to have sex with each other because we were both virgins, but we'd always hug really close and always talk on the phone for hours.

Lionel was my first boyfriend encounter, and we really did like each other. It was sort of cute in a sense because my sister's boyfriend (which was his older brother), Markus, used to come over with Lionel every time, so it was like we were double-dating when we'd all hook up. My oldest sister was really into her boyfriend, Marcus. She really did love him and had a big heart for him. Marcus and Lionel were really wonderful boys. They were very respectable and very quiet that you would not have thought that they were brought up in our neighborhood. They both were such gentlemen to us that when they saw us, they would hold the gates open when we took walks around the neighborhood and held our hand.

They always greeted us with a hug and a kiss on the cheek, and they always respectfully greeted our mother. They were always dressed so proper with their button-up shirts tucked in their slacks and dress shoes, as we used to call them, church shoes. Marcus and Lionel both attended private schools. They lived with both of their parents, which was a rarity in our neighborhood because they were growing up with their mother and father. Their mother and father were both Christians, and they always went to church on Sunday. They were very adamant about their sons doing Bible study at home all the time. I remember Marcus and Lionel would make fun of their Bible study sessions to us, and we used to laugh all the time about it. But they really respected their parents and loved them. They were their parents' only kids; their parents were an older couple, maybe in their late forties. They lived around the corner from our house so they were never that far away, so whenever we'd call them to come over, they'd show up almost instantly.

One day, my sister went to call Marcus so that he and Lionel could come over. I noticed that she started looking very sad while she was on the phone while calling him. I didn't hear the conversation that she was having on the phone because I just walked past her trying my best to mind my own business. I figured maybe they were having their first fight, so I didn't want to be nosey and I kept on my way. After a while of being on the phone, my sister screamed and yelled my name to come to her. When I went to the living room to see what she wanted, I saw her run to the couch and put two pillows over her head and started screaming and crying, saying, "Why, why, why!" I didn't know why she was crying and was so sad. I thought that maybe she and Marcus had broken up. I didn't ask her anything or say anything and waited for her to calm down to tell me what had happened. She told me to sit next to her on the couch, and when I sat down next to her, she started hugging me and rocking back and forth.

I knew she was upset with Marcus because she kept saying over and over again, "Why'd you do that, Marcus! Why'd you do that!" I was a little upset at first too because I was being selfish in my thinking at that moment while she was upset. All that I could think about was if she's breaking up with Marcus, then I'll never get to see Lionel again because he can't come over here without his big brother. I honestly didn't want her and Marcus to break up because he was a really nice guy to my sister, and to top that off, I knew I wouldn't be able to have my relationship with his little brother any longer. After my sister was allowed to finally calm herself down, she finally told me the unfortunate, tragic news. A tragedy had taken place with Marcus, and my sister just did not know how to tell me about it (as she couldn't handle the sad news herself). The best way that she could tell me about what had happened to Marcus was to first reminisce about all the wonderful things that he did for her and the fun that they had together.

At first, nothing that she was saying to me made any sense because I knew about most of the wonderful things that he did for her and how great their relationship was. I was around them most of the time, and she always told me about the fun things that they did together, even for the times I wasn't around them. I was sort of confused, but I just wanted her to talk and let it out because if she was really breaking up with him, I knew that had to be hard for her. So after she talked to me about the great relationship that they had together, she finally broke the bad news to me that Marcus had accidentally shot and killed himself playing with their father's gun. I couldn't believe what I was hearing.

I had questions, so I asked her, "Are you sure? Is he dead? Who told you this?" She told me that his father answered the phone when she called him and told her that Marcus and Lionel were in their station wagon messing with the gun that they had taken out of the house. Marcus was trying to figure out how to take out the clip and the gun went off and shot him in the chest. She then told me that his father said that he would let her know a date and time when his funeral will be held to call back and get the information. I couldn't believe what she told me; it was not registering in my mind that Marcus was dead. I felt so sad about what had happened. We both cried that whole night because we had just seen him the day before that happened. Our mother told us that she saw what had happened to him on the news, and she gave us big hugs and told us that he was in heaven with God and not to worry.

All I kept wondering about was if we would have called them over that day to our house to come see us, that would have never happened. I felt so sad about what happened that I stopped talking to Lionel and didn't call him anymore because I didn't know what to say to him. Nothing like that has ever happened to me before, and I was afraid that I would say all the wrong things to him. His brother was his closest and only best friend, and he looked up to him. He always said that when he grew up, he wanted to be like Marcus because he was really smart in school and was a very handsome, cool young man. Lionel was a great kid too; he just didn't have his big brother's coolness and handsome looks. He was a very smart kid in school, and he was also so shy.

Years later, I ran across Lionel on Seventy-Ninth in Oakland, close by where he lived. I wasn't doing so well because at this point in my life, I was on drugs and living on the streets, and when I saw Lionel, I was shocked because he didn't look like himself and I could tell that he was heavily doing drugs. He looked very bummish, his clothes were dirty, he smelled really funky, and his hair looked like it hadn't been combed in days. When we first saw each other, we hugged each other, and he cried and told me why didn't I call him back when his brother had passed away. I explained to him that I didn't know what to say to him and I felt that maybe he did not want to talk to anybody after what had happened. He said that after he lost his brother, he lost his mind and he was never the same after that happened. And when he told me that, I looked at Lionel up and down and saw that he was still affected by his brother's death.

The Ducktails

But after time grew, my mother eventually moved out of our home from our house on Seventy-Sixth due to the dramas that started to occur with the neighbors, and she was trying so hard to live up to her aunt's expectations that it all became too stressful for her. We were back at square one at my grandmother's house on Ninety-Sixth. It was hard to understand why we ended up having to move from that house, but all I know is that my mother was not happy especially because she was in the heart of what she needed to escape. As far as I thought that she would be okay because she was able to live in front of her siblings with her family and the neighbors were cool and they became friends, but in all reality, my mother was cooped up in her own little hell that I didn't realize at that moment. She really needed to be somewhere where she was away from drugs and temptation and peer pressure and anywhere that reminded her of a bad place, and even though it felt good to me, I was not in my mother's shoes to understand that she was in the exact place where she did not need to be. She was confused on what she was going to do about her new journey, but she felt like she had to get away from that area.

It was all a mess. After a while, it seemed like that house that we were living in on Seventy-Sixth was tainted, especially because she was beat up by a drug dealer in that house, she was in peer pressure and seduced by her brother-in-law, she was forced to do whatever it took to get money for us to be able to afford to take care of our house which caused her to do the things that she did not want to do, or kids were on and all things and see things you should have seen at that house, and the list goes on and on about why she felt like she needed to make that move that she made. The first thing for my mother to do, I guess, for her was to go back to her mother's house to stay there. There were a bunch of adults living there because everyone is very adult and grown-up and some also have kids of their own now. So by it being a four-bedroom house with two bathrooms—two bedrooms up top of the house, one bathroom downstairs with two bedrooms with a bathroom—and both floors having living room areas, now these places are being shared with three different families in the house. At this point, once we moved back into my grandmother's house, everything was so different.

My uncle who had his son staying there with him at the time was the uncle at the moment who drank heavily and would always pick arguments with people around the house when he didn't have enough money to get booze or drugs. He didn't work an actual, real job, but he did fly jobs around the neighborhood, like clean sweep people's yards or pick fruits or vegetables with some of the farmers in the area. He did little things like that or storerooms for people and they pay them with a beer and maybe five dollars. So whenever he does not have enough money to go get him any more beer or crack, he will pick a fight with whoever he thinks is the happiest. That's how I saw it. He was very evil in that house at this point; he was always starting trouble and was very loud, very violent, and very obnoxious. A lot of times, other uncles or aunts would have to try and contain him, and if that didn't work, they will call the police to come, and the police will usually come hours later after they've been called and they would take him in the car so they had him overnight until he sobered up and send him back the next day.

My brother, at the time, was the same age as his son.

I always felt that my uncle was very jealous of my mother's son because my brother had long hair, and he started trying to grow his son's hair. Back in these times, there was this hairdo called the high-top fade in the ducktail in the back. That type of hairdo was a kind of hairdo where it would be a nice afro body shape cut at the top and say ditto around the middle part of the head. That would be loose hung down like bangs or cut in a small square shape and braided into one long braid. The longer your ducktail braid, the fancier or good you had it. So at this time, my mother had to cut my brother's hair, and my brother's hair was fairly long, so she gave him the style that left him the ducktail at the back of his hair. His ducktail hair that was styled on his head went down to the middle of his back. On the other hand, my uncle that's usually the one that gets drunk and goes off on everybody for no reason, his son had the same age as my mother's son, had a ducktail and his ducktail was a quarter of the length of my brother's. That's hell.

So a lot of times, when neighbors or people would come over to visit and they would see my little brother, they would always compliment my mother about how beautiful he was as a little boy and that he had really long hair because of his ducktail length. My brother said they gave him a lot of attention, especially with the older women when they came by. This particular uncle lacked the type of quality where women would adore him, so he always had a hard time getting women, and one of the reasons why a lot of the people in the house thought that he was so angry was because he was not putting out with women as he wished he should have.

But back to the situation at hand, his son who was the same age as my little brother did not get as many compliments as my brother was getting. So a couple of weeks went by and he's noticing how women would come over and compliment my brother, complimenting my mother on having such a beautiful son with a long ducktail hair and that he was cute, and after he couldn't take it anymore, my uncle picked a fight with my mother for no apparent reason. We were in the kitchen, and he looked over at my little brother who was every bit about four or five years old and said, "Your son ain't sh——— with his light-skinned a———." And when he said that, everybody who heard him in the house, including myself, were stunned that he would say something like that to his own sister about his own nephew who was only just a four-year-old kid. I guess his jealousy just got the best of him, and he just let whatever he was feeling and thinking loose. So my mother, turning red, looked over at my uncle and said, "What did you just say about my son?"

And he repeated himself and looked at her straight to her face and said, "Your son ain't sh——— with his light-skinned a———, he ain't all that!"

And so my mother's skin started to turn copper-penny red while looking very sad and angry at the same time, and said back to him, "What problems do you have with me, Ronnie? I've never done nothing wrong to you! I don't even say anything to you! I don't bother you. My kids help out every day around this house and clean up after y'all! What you and your son do all the time is go around here, pick fights with everybody, and cuss people out! You don't even care enough about me to even be nice, and you know what I'm going through right now!"

My uncle responded back to her, "Yeah, b———, I don't give a d———! Take your d——— kids and get the hell out of here! You should have never moved back here in the first place!"

I was watching this whole scene play out before my eyes, and I ended up getting so upset that I wanted to hit my uncle and run! I did not like how he was talking to my mother, and I did not like how he was talking about my baby brother. Other people in the house were getting upset but didn't want him messing with them and their kids, so they did not say anything. They just let their sister and brother go at it. After the two finished exchanging some offensive words, everyone continued eating while all the kids in the house were in the kitchen, eating at the kitchen table. Meanwhile, after that altercation took place, I was so angry and sad about that whole incident that I lost my appetite. My mother was still very upset, so she went outside on the porch to try and calm down. So while my mother was outside calming down, trying to contain herself while being upset, my uncle rushed downstairs to his lounge area (where he used to live), rushed back up the stairs really fast with a fury in his eyes carrying what appeared to be scissors in his hand.

My uncle walked over to my little brother while he was sitting at the kitchen table eating his dinner and grabbed his long braid and cut it off! The braid of hair that my uncle cut off of my brother's head was a hairstyle at that time called a ducktail. Men of color were wearing that hairstyle back then as a way of saving a piece of their hair on their head to show off the length of how long their hair would be if it hadn't been cut or shaved. The longer the ducktail, the higher the props you received. My mother has been growing and saving my little brother's ducktail since his very first haircut when he was two years old. My uncle (who cut off my brother's ducktail) was growing his son's ducktail too, but his son's ducktail was very short in length.

All the kids in the kitchen screamed, even his son! We screamed because we were terrified of why he did that, and we were just scared because we didn't know if he was going to take those same scissors and hurt somebody with them because he was acting irate. That was a very scary moment. My brother started to cry, and he looked over and saw his braids lying on the floor on the side of him. My uncle looked directly at my baby brother and said, "That's what your ass did, ha-ha, now you don't have s—— on your head!"

My baby brother was sitting there, screaming and crying, and me and my sisters were going off on my uncle, cursing at him, yelling at him, screaming and telling him how jealous he was of our brother because his son's hair wasn't long. While we were going off on our uncle, our mother came in. I guess one of the other brothers went outside on the porch to tell her what happened. So when she came in, she couldn't believe what she saw!

She saw her son's nice haircut ruined and his hair that she had been growing since he was a baby that was left over in the form of a ducktail was completely gone and cut off and lying on the floor next to her crying son. My mother screamed and yelled and went for a pot and went to go to chase and hurt my uncle, but her other brothers and sisters were able to hold her down and contain her and said, "Don't worry about it, we're just going to call the police on him and get him out of the house for tonight until he calms down." My mother didn't care about what they were saying because she was so upset about what happened to her son that she picked up my brother after they let her go and she left, and I don't remember where she went but it had to be about three hours that she was gone.

So when my mother came back, she was upset, she was crying, she was talking to my grandmother. I don't remember what she was telling her, but all I remember is that the very next day, my mother was making a whole bunch of phone calls and she wouldn't tell us what she was doing but we didn't bother her. We just continued to go outside and play with our friends and just continue on with our normal day as kids. So after four days have passed, I came home from school and my mom, my brother, and my baby sister weren't there. Normally, they would be there at the house when I would get out of school, but on this day, the house seemed very empty and very quiet and no one said nothing to me so I thought nothing of it.

Day five goes by and I haven't seen my mother, my brother, or my baby sister. Now I was starting to get worried as I was walking home from school telling myself that if I don't see my mother when I get out of school, then something must not be right. And so nobody's telling me about it. So I got to the house and I noticed that my brother, my mother, and my baby sister still weren't there. So I got curious and decided to go ahead and ask my grandmother if she saw my mom and did she know where she was with my sister and my brother. My grandmother gave me a look of confusion and said, "I don't know where she went." All I know is she took my baby brother and sister with her.

So I said, "Is she coming back?"

My grandmother looked at me and said, "Baby, I don't know. I hope so. I hope she didn't run away because she was really upset and I did see her take a couple of bags and her purse, but I don't know. She hasn't called, and she hasn't come back."

So now day six goes by and still no mother, no baby brother, and no baby sister. I started crying and walking toward the backyard to sit on the back steps to get my thoughts together. I sat there and asked myself, *Did my mother really just leave me, Chantel, and Tasha here at our grandmother's house and take our baby brother and sister with her?* Then I started to ask myself, *Maybe she's staying with a friend around the corner because she doesn't want to see Lonzo because she might go off on him.* Then I also thought, *Okay, well, maybe she's just one adult then being somewhere with a man and she took my little brother and sister with her because she didn't want to leave them here with Ronnie.*

After clear thought and prayers, as I sat there on my grandmother's back steps, I had finally come to the conclusion, after a couple of hours went by and I didn't hear my mother go through the door with my baby sister and brother running to the backyard to find me, that my mother was gone. She left! I went to my grandmother's bedroom, and I hugged her and I cried and I said, "Mommy, did my mama leave us here?"

And my grandmother looked at me and said, "I guess so because it's been a few days and she hasn't called me and I haven't seen her and the babies."

And I asked my grandmother, "Mommy, is she going to get me, Chantel, and Tasha?"

And she said, "Willa Wonka, don't worry about it. I'm sure she's not going to leave you for a long time. You can stay here with me and just sleep in my bed so that way you don't feel sad every time you think about your mom because I know she didn't mean to leave you on purpose."

And I started crying. I couldn't believe that my mother really left me like that or my other sisters for that matter. My mother was not aware of what my cousin was doing to us.

All I kept thinking about was, *Oh no, I'm back here again and it's fun at this moment with my grandmother. I feel safe, but my cousin knows how to sneak me out of her room without waking her up. I hope he doesn't come back here, so for now, I'm just going to have fun with my cousins and help my grandmother and do my best at school and try to stay out of trouble so that I don't upset none of the other rooms that's here so I can have somewhere to live.* Those were my thoughts at that moment because I was confused and I was concerned and worried about being molested all over again by my cousin.

Weeks have gone by, and I haven't seen my cousin at that house, which was a bonus because I was actually able to have fun with my cousins and play with them and go to school and got me some new friends and new friends in the neighborhood we were able to go play with, so I was always busy playing with kids and doing errands for grown-ups in the house and doing my chores so that way I could have sworn that I would be able to eat and not have to worry about the grown-ups in the house feeling like I was in the way and eating for free because my mother wasn't around and wasn't paying for my stay there.

I tried to make the best out of the whole situation and not worry so much about my mother being gone with my baby brother and baby sister. Because I miss them so much, I did my best to tune out the stress from thinking about them. I continued to pray that my cousin stays gone wherever he was, to play, continue to do chores around the house, go to school, do store errands for adults in the house, hoping they would pay me for it with a quarter or with some chips or something that they bought which was cool too! I was humble and I was hungry, so whatever I was getting to eat, I was happy about it and I'm not complaining about it. I was also happy at this point because my grandmother actually let me lie in the bed with her on her side of her bed, so there was one for me there and I didn't have to sleep on the floor. No signs of my cousin was around, but here and there, my uncle who was crazy and loud, and another aunt did not like me because I was black. So she called me blackie because I was dark-skinned in the house even though she was dark-skinned too. I never understood that, but I was just able to just deal with all the stress because it could have been worse and I could have been, like, homeless on the streets or dead, so they didn't bother me. I didn't bother them, and if they did bother me, I just got over it. My mother had it the worst probably because she helped raise her siblings and she was the oldest of the thirteen children that my grandmother and grandfather bore. But she never got that respect as the oldest in that house when she was staying there with all five of her kids. She got a lot of heat because she had a lot of kids and we were extra mouths to feed, so people did give her a hard time, and they gave her kids a hard time too.

The only people that really truly seemed to care and not give my mother such a hard time were her three brothers, who were the more responsible adults—my three uncles that were great providers for the house—and my grandmother. One of my uncles was not living at the house. He was living somewhere else, and another aunt had married and moved out of the home. My sister was able to move with her friend who lived next door, and her parents were her adopted parents and they were the landlord and owners of the apartment complex. So my sister had it made living there in that house because it was really beautiful. She got to share a room with her friend, and she was able to wear nice clothes and go to school and fight being dropped off with her boyfriend's parents. My other sister was able to live with my great aunt who lives in the hills in a nice big home in the Oakland Hills, and she was living really good, eating good, dressing really pretty, hair was always combed, and she was always clean, and it was a beautiful thing.

But as for me, I lived at my grandmother's house. I guess nobody wanted me to live with them, so my only choice was to stay at my grandmother's house without any of my sisters being there. I used to get so jealous and sad because when I would go to where my sisters were staying, I noticed that they had their own drawers, their own beds, and their hair was always nice and neat. They had nice clothes. They were eating good food in the house where they were able to just go to the kitchen and get snacks when they wanted, yet on the other hand, I was in dirty clothes, sleeping on the side of my grandmother's bed, and I was not eating snacks all day or eating good. I was basically going to school with my hair nappy, no hair stuff to work with to make my hair cute, but I always busted the best that I could so that way I didn't look too bad at school.

I was hand-washing my clothes in the bathtub when the washing machine broke in my grandmother's house, so that was hard. So a lot of my clothes were not 100 percent clean, but they weren't 100 percent dirty either. My clothes looked as if they were dingy and stained, but it was the result of me trying to hand-wash them so I can have clean underwear and clean socks to wear to school. Struggle is real. I was not the cute kid that my mother had with the nice light skin in the pretty long good hair. I was more of the rugged one, the dark one with the nappy edges and thick long hair. I had that, but my skin complexion was a bother to a lot of people for some reason. For a long time, people around the house was calling me blackie, and I hated it every time they called me that and I believe a couple of my aunts knew it but still called me that anyway. I never understood why older people in that house would not look at me. I was just a kid and not just someone that's walking around in that house. Sometimes I felt so uncomfortable being there that I felt that I was in the way.

The Final Straw

After searching high and low for my mother, I finally found her at a shelter in San Francisco, which she eventually got back in touch with a man she was dating before out there because he was out there too. She left the shelter and moved in with him to a two-bedroom house on Seventy-Second Rusdale in East Oakland. So of course, my oldest sister and I tagged along to live in that house together. We loved living with our mother and wanted to help keep an eye out on our younger siblings. My sister Chantel continued to stay with her best friend who lived at the apartments next door to Big Momma's house. The house that my mother and her boyfriend moved in to was comfortable, quiet, and clean. Unfortunately, the man whom she was in a relationship with indulged in drugs, and they both got high on some occasions.

On this strange particular day, they had a male friend over with his friend, and I believe the man that he brought with him wanted to experiment with drugs. They must've given him too much of a hit because this man who was six-foot-one and built in stature came running out of the room, moving fast like a guinea pig, back and forth up and down the hallway. It frightened me so much that I hid on the side of the couch. I've never seen anything like that before. Thankfully, my brother and sister were asleep in their room, where the man did not go. My oldest sister wasn't there that night. I got up from off the floor behind the couch to try and run in the room to be with my siblings, but by the time I got up, the man's friend and my mom calmed him down. He was calm for a few minutes, then all of a sudden, he started shaking and taking his clothes off and ended up having nothing on at all! Everyone was concerned for him, but my mother's boyfriend was not helping the situation. He just stayed in the room during the whale fiasco. So my mother helped put the man in the bathtub to run cold water over him, and it worked. He was calmed and back to his normal self after a long forty-minute struggle.

After I ran to the back room to check on the little ones, I heard a commotion happening in the front area of the house. To my surprise, as I opened the door, I saw the man holding my mother's boyfriend by the neck with his fist balled up and cocked back. I left out the room and closed the door behind me and asked everyone what was going on. They were telling me to go back in the room, but the man looked over at me and said, "Hey, kid! Nothing to worry about, go back to your room!"

My mother yelled at her boyfriend and said, "Dan, give this man his money back so he can go!"

The other male friend yelled the same thing to Dan, but he kept saying that he didn't have his money.

I yelled to Dan too, "If you got this man's money, give it back!" but he still kept insisting that he didn't have it.

The man's friend came over to me and gave me a ten-dollar bill and told me to go to the room because it was about to get ugly.

I didn't know what he meant by that, but I was praying, hoping for my mother to not get in the way.

So I asked the man in my most frantic voice, "He doesn't think my mom took his money, does he?"

He responded back, "My name is Davy, and I'm so sorry you have to see this, but your mother's boyfriend took my friend's money, and he just wants what is his so we can leave, but he won't cough it up! We know your mother had nothing to do with it because she was trying to help us the whole time that my friend was 'illin. So no worries, sweetheart. I know you're concerned about your mother, but we're not going to do anything to her, she's safe, she's just trying to talk him into giving my friend his money. Now can you please go back to your room? This is a grown-up situation."

As Davy was introducing himself to me and explaining the situation to me, I saw the man punch Dan so hard in the face that I knew right then and there that 911 would have to be called. I think he broke Dan's nose because I heard a pop sound, and my mother started screaming for them to just leave and not to hurt her boyfriend. Thank God that he intervened because the two men left before it could've gotten worse. That was probably going to be the death of Dan if they wouldn't have left. Dan was left on the floor, bleeding, waiting for the paramedics to come. My mother was so shaken up and upset. It was horrible, and after that happened, my mother had discussed plans to move and leave Dan alone. The question still remained, "Did he take that man's money?" I guess we'll never know. As time moved on and all the crazy calmed down, I went to visit my grandmother and to see my cousins since it's been a while.

It was early when I caught the bus to go visit. It ended up getting late, so I decided to stay the night and leave back home in the morning. By this time, I was twelve years old and started menstruating at this age. I was hanging in my grandmother's kitchen, talking with my cousins, and was in good spirits and hadn't seen my older cousin around that whole day. That was why I didn't mind staying overnight versus trying to catch the bus and leave so late at night. It had to be around ten o'clock at night when I found myself alone in the kitchen, waiting for my other cousins to come back. I went over to the kitchen sink to make me some water, and I saw someone from my peripheral vision staring at me from the downstairs staircase.

My heart dropped because when I turned my head to look and make sure that I wasn't seeing things, unfortunately, I wasn't seeing things. It was my older cousin staring at me with his head peeking through the staircase handle. He scared the living daylights out of me! He looked so creepy because he blended in well with the staircase. As I was walking back to sit at the kitchen table, he started again, "Psst! Aye, Willia, come here!"

At this point in my life, I've been through enough blues and seen enough that I was not going to let him destroy me any longer.

I stood up to him and said, "I'm not going anywhere in any more rooms with you, cousin. I am twelve years old and have started my period. You cannot touch me anymore, so please stop asking me to come downstairs or anywhere else with you because I'm not ever going!"

I thought by me getting loud and putting him on blast would work, but that just made him beg more while he was still hiding behind the staircase handle. It annoyed me so bad that I'd rather take my chance with strangers in the streets that late at night just so I could get back home than lay with him ever again. I stepped out in faith, knowing that God would see me home safely and in one piece, so my worries left my conscience. I left toward the front door and told everyone goodbye and caught the eleven o'clock bus to go back home. Someone was confused and yelled while I was walking down the street, "Wait, cousin, I thought you were spending the night, where are you going?"

I replied back, "I've got to go! See y'all tomorrow."

I thank God that he didn't follow me because I would have panicked. And I would have tried my best to fight him off. At this age, I was fully developed with breasts, pubic hairs, and menstruating; there was just no way I could see myself laying up with my cousin. Once I safely made it home, I noticed an aunt-in-law was there talking with my oldest sister, having a fun and funny conversation. So I thought I'd join in and have a good laugh, the good Lord knew I needed one.

After many chuckles, my aunt-in-law revealed to me that she was dating a family member of ours but not the one that she shared a child with. My sister and I looked at each other confused, like, who could she be talking about? I thought that it was strange that she was dating a man in our family that isn't who she was originally with before. But we didn't want to judge her, so in anticipation and excitement, we asked her who was the other relative of ours that she was dating and blushing over. She then revealed who it was, and my sister and I looked at each in dismay and disbelief.

Not because of the situation but because of the person she told us it was. All I could think of in my head was, *He sure does get around, up, down, high, and low!* Not only did he sleep with most girls in the neighborhood and even his own little cousins, but he's sleeping with my uncle's baby's momma too? Wowed me in the head. This man could never get enough. I was blown back because she started talking about how he romanced her and caressed her as if she's the only one he wants and is into. Not even knowing what just happened to me and why I was getting in the house that late. My sister and I couldn't help but look at each other in pure disgust, and after so many times of that same reaction on our faces without telling her a word about him, she stopped us right in our tracks!

With no hesitation, she asked, "Why do every time I say something about your cousin, you two keep lookin' like that? Oh no! I know that look!" She immediately tried so hard to drag the truth out of us, a secret we've been holding in for so many years, not even our mother knew. Finally! She dragged the truth out of us because she was getting angry at the moment and saying to us that if we don't tell her, she was going to tell our mom. So we told her everything that he did to us, and I cried because I had to hear my sister's experience and it was a nightmare to hear! I let them both know why I left my grandmother's house and what happened, and our aunt-in-law went on to tell us that maybe he wanted us to bear his children because that was bound to happen if we didn't tell on him.

So we went to wake up my mom, and I told her everything. My mother's reaction was the opposite of how I thought she was going to react. She screamed and jumped out of her bed and yelled, "I'm going to kill him! Not my daughters!"

We tried to calm her down, but I think she blacked out! She ran to the kitchen and grabbed a big butcher's knife and ran out of the door with no shoes on, in her pj's, walking toward my grandmother's house, chanting that she was going to kill him! We couldn't stop her. We chased her down three blocks on East Fourteenth Street as she headed on her way as fast as she could to Big Momma's house. Our aunt-in-law told us to stay with her and that she's running back to the house to call the police. When she met back up with us, she alarmed us that the police were on their way and told my mother to try her best to calm down, that he's not worth her going to prison for killing him. My mother was so upset, still screaming and crying. I felt so bad for her because she was really hurt. We were finally able to get her to stop and put her shoes on that my aunt had brought from the house.

She was crying her heart out and then kept saying, "I'm so sorry, y'all! I didn't know! I didn't know! Why y'all didn't tell me sooner!"

I chuckled and said, "Because this is why," trying to be sarcastic to get her to calm down. It didn't work. After she caught her breath, she got back up walking as fast as she could back on her way there. Thanks be to God that when we arrived, there were four police cars there with our cousin in the back of one of the police units, so to my relief, he'd already surrendered before my mother got to him. My mother banged the police car and window where he was sitting and gave him a piece of her emotions.

I was also grateful that my aunt took the butcher's knife before we approached the police officers. While we were being questioned by the officers, we could hear rants from my grandmother's porch that we were not allowed to go back there ever again. I heard shouts of anger toward us, and that broke my heart to pieces because they made us out to be the enemies. That instant feeling of being an outcast and neglect from something that happened to me that was not my fault. Then a cloud of guilt came over me. I beat myself up for a few days, telling myself that I should've not said anything.

After some serious counseling and therapy, my attorney gave me the good news that I didn't have to go to court and testify on the stand because he surrendered himself and pleaded guilty and was being sentenced as we spoke. That was so relieving because God knows I didn't want to take the stand and say in full description the events. I was twelve years old, and that would've been too much for me at that time. I still wonder 'til this very day, had I not spoken up, what would've happened?

This was only the beginning.

About the Author

How Could I Forget series is written in this compelling story based on real-life events by author Alicia Hutcherson, also known as Willa Wonka. She is the product of an unstable and complicated childhood, adolescence, and adulthood that had such an impact on her life until God saved her before destruction would befall her. This first part of the series that she wrote takes a look into what it was like for her while growing up in a dysfunctional and unordinary childhood.

Alicia Hutcherson is now a survivor of a dreadful past. She is now a full-time devoted wife and mother who bore eleven children, of which ten are living. By God's will, she is now a published author as her full-time job. As a child, she always wanted to be a housewife and mother of ten children that she could love and care for. That was always her dream and goal in life. Once she became a young adult, she also wanted to help people, however and whenever she could. She faced many horrific obstacles during her lifetime before her dreams became a reality. Life threw bricks at her whichever way they could, but she always managed to make a shelter with those bricks. Life threw her lemons, but she always made iced lemon tea with those lemons. She's seen death stare her straight in the eyes, which put so much fear in her that God was her only hope for change. Once she completely learned about God in his entirety, she feared him more than death! Her love, faith, and trust in God gave her hope and encouragement to not look back, to keep going, and to never give up.

Life was never an easy task, but somehow, Alicia always seemed to manage, and when asked 'til this very day how does she do it? She would always respond with "It's all God!"

Alicia Hutcherson survived challenges and turmoil that some wouldn't have survived. Her strength comes from a heavenly dwelling.

CPSIA information can be obtained
at www.ICGtesting.com
Printed in the USA
LVHW040821190621
690567LV00005B/390